Quarterly Essay

CONTENTS

iii   Introduction *Peter Craven*

1   RABBIT SYNDROME
       Australia and America
       Don Watson

60   THE OPPORTUNIST Correspondence
       John Birmingham, Paul Bongiorno, Christopher Pearson, Tony Walker,
       Guy Rundle

89   Contributors

Quarterly Essay is published four times a year by Black Inc., an imprint of Schwartz Publishing Pty Ltd
Publisher: Morry Schwartz

ISBN 1 86395 115 6

Subscriptions (4 issues): $34.95 a year within Australia incl. GST (Institutional subs. $40). Outside Australia $70. Payment may be made by Mastercard, Visa or Bankcard, or by cheque made out to Schwartz Publishing. Payment includes postage and handling.

Correspondence and subscriptions should be addressed to the Editor at:
Black Inc.
Level 3, 167 Collins St
Melbourne VIC 3000
Australia
Phone: 61 3 9654 2000
Fax: 61 3 9654 2290
Email: quarterlyessay@blackincbooks.com

Editor: Peter Craven
Management: Silvia Kwon
Assistant Editor: Chris Feik
Publishing Assistant: Sophy Williams
Publicity: Meredith Kelly
Design: Guy Mirabella
Printer: McPherson's Printing Group
Image: Mike Bowers/*The Australian Financial Review*

Quarterly Essay aims to present significant contributions to political, intellectual and cultural debate. It is a magazine in extended pamphlet form and by publishing in each issue a single writer of at least 20,000 words we hope to mediate between the limitations of the newspaper column, where there is the danger that evidence and argument can be swallowed up by the form, and the kind of full-length study of a subject where the only readership is a necessarily specialised one. *Quarterly Essay* aims for the attention of the committed general reader. Although it is a periodical which wants subscribers, each number of the journal will be the length of a short book because we want our writers to have the opportunity to speak to the broadest possible audience without condescension or populist shortcuts. *Quarterly Essay* wants to get away from the tyranny that space limits impose in contemporary journalism and we will be giving our essayists the space to express the evidence for their views and those who disagree with them the chance to reply at whatever length is necessary. *Quarterly Essay* will not be confined to politics but it will be centrally concerned with it. We are not interested in occupying any particular point on the political map and we hope to bring our readership the widest range of political and cultural opinion which is compatible with truth-telling, style and command of the essay form.

INTRODUCTION

This is not an essay about Australia locked in the embrace of America as the two nations go to war over terrorism in Afghanistan to find the ghostly trail of bin Laden. It is not in the first instance an essay about foreign policy at all. Don Watson, the fourth of our quarterly essayists, has been closer to the centre of power than any of his predecessors but this is in some respects the most literary of the *Quarterly Essays* so far – a ruminative, sceptical look at the received idea of our relationship with the United States which is tinged with a melancholy whimsy and everywhere invokes the ghost of the ancient Australian irony and stoicism which Watson is inclined to suggest has vanished from the earth and never amounted to much anyway (not in an imaginative landscape that includes Lincoln and Sherman and Judy Garland and the reimagining of history by the great John Ford).

Don Watson was trained as an historian and influenced both by Greg Dening's variety of anthropological relativism and by the idealism and trailing banners of Manning Clark whom he defended with some subtlety as a case of history reborn as farce. Watson went on to become a *farceur* himself, albeit a politico-historical one, when he became one of the authors of the Max Gillies show. And then, famously – not without drawing obvious comment from Andrew Peacock – he became the speechwriter and then the advisor of Paul Keating.

Rabbit Syndrome is an attempt to put Australia and the culture of anxiety about Australia in a globalist perspective while still retaining an Australian accent, no matter how swish the suit is. And in Don Watson's case the verbal cut is as elegant as the national voice is distinctive and modulated even if part of the trick with this partly satirical essay is to suggest that Australia is the arse-end of the earth. At least as much so, he insinuates, as it is "the best country on earth" which is one of the abiding myths he does not so much repudiate as deconstruct, tracing fine lines of paradox and forever shadowing any posited value with the tracings of its opposite.

The man from Gippsland who went on to ventriloquise first for a great Melbourne comedian and then for a Sydney streetfighter tempted by the spectre of statesmanship is one of those voices who has an affinity for Hibberd, for Furphy, for Lawson. Watson's vision of Australia – which takes the form of constantly refusing to believe in an Australian vision – is in that line of melancholy scepticism which is central to whatever tradition we have.

Hence his peculiar relation to that old Australian chestnut, that old Australian cliché, A.A. Phillips's Cultural Cringe. Watson's position is that of someone who says that he has nothing against the Cultural Cringe if there's something worth cringing about in our culture. And before the charge is laid too readily against him – as it will be – it is worth remembering that Phillips, fifty years ago, wrote in a context where Australian writing, Australian culture, was liable to be derogated whereas the opposite is likely to be the case today.

In any case Don Watson is addressing himself to the predicament which Henry James dubbed "the Complex Fate", apropos of America. What do you do when everything that feeds your imagination, that defines your sensibility, comes from a world elsewhere? For the cultivated nineteenth-century American paradoxically occupying the site of his nation's great Renaissance, this was Europe. For Watson, with a complex irony that is the opposite of naïve, it is America.

He devotes some time to tracing the archetypal divisions, for an Australian of the boomer generation, between Britain and America. He notes the limitations of the American product (the supposed lack of the sense of humour we share with the Ealing comedies and John Cleese) and then, notwithstanding their grandstanding war movies, the enveloping majesty and seductiveness, the power and the glory of an American culture without which we would not be what we are. Indeed the way we imagine ourselves would be inconceivable in a quite literal sense.

Here we come close to the tendency towards historical idealism that is central to Watson's cast of mind. Not the lofty-minded pursuit of ideals (he has little truck with that) but the deflected philosophical idealism that says the way we think and believe and mythologise the world has a significance and an interest that material conditions and political events cannot in themselves capture or disclose.

Hence the centrality which this essay gives to the "Rabbit" novels of John Updike. On the one hand they represent for Watson a kind of pinnacle of contemporary literary achievement which Australian writing can barely hope to match (how could the social conditions combine to register this kind of book?) and on the other they disclose a matchless social panorama at every point. This may seem like a self-fulfilling prophecy, whichever way you look at it: only Americans can produce writing this great and what's great about this novel is the America it represents. But it would be wrong to dismiss Watson with a too-easy theory, a too-easy logic. At one level he is dramatising the fact that powerful American culture speaks to us in ways our own generally does not but what is most interesting here is that this leads him to his central move – Rabbit can be taken (the author chooses to take him) as a metaphor of Australia.

So Rabbit, this powerful representation of American hopelessness, is also a representation (in the mind's eye of the essayist) of us. What may be disputed in the given instance is liable to be true allegorically and by general extension, and so it goes through the widening circles of social and political paradox which Don Watson traces.

America, however flawed its mighty empire may be, is a more benign empire than any other: it is certainly more benign than the totalitarianism it opposed. And, besides, it has always had the capacity, the vitality to sell counter-images of the world (images that counter its own domination) to a cultural colony like Australia. Hence the counterculture itself, which had Australian Leftists in a haze of drugs and sex, espousing like their American doubles (their brothers, their sisters, with their ever-potent market) the bully-boys of Communism as if they were icons of freedom and pleasure and grace.

And, yes, America for all its glory and its relative benignity is also a ghastly society, in touch with nightmares of vengeance and bloodymindedness that little old gradualist Australian cannot dream of or can only dream of by proxy. Australia, that convict success story, has never carried on about freedom, because it took it for granted, but then it also takes for granted its own status (mythological in its own eyes) as a low-rent paradise.

Watson is a sceptic and a pessimist. He knows that the digger mentality is dead and gone and that it cannot be resurrected. The things Australians like to think of themselves as fighting for, the sacred story that is part of our mythology of forty-hour weeks and mighty union movements and the lowest possible gap between rich and poor in the context of a high standard of living: these things are dead or dying all around us. He does not elaborately bemoan this but his tone is poignant with an elegiac note that he holds back whenever he touches on it. His substantive point, however, is that at a certain moment, rightly or wrongly (no prize for guessing when or under whose influence), Australia took irreversible steps towards becoming a harder, a more "American" society than it would ever have dreamt of. It had always been half-American in its head, but not so long ago it set about eliminating those features of its politico-economic ethos that made it collectivist, particularist, a marsupial social democracy with a shared ethos for which the "fair go" and "mateship" were shorthands. These shorthands live on as archaeological trace elements in the world view of the current Prime Minister, even though he, as much as his predecessor, has kicked against the structures that might underlie any such consensus.

Rabbit Syndrome is not primarily an essay about foreign policy and it is still less an apologia for foreign policy under Keating. But it is clearly the work of a man who believes that a policy of seeing ourselves as part of Asia, of adhering to a republican spirit and preferably a Republican practice, and preserving a "relaxed erectness of carriage" in friendly but not subservient dealings with the United States, was the only way to go. The trouble with being America's deputy is that sooner or later you're told to knuckle down and do your dirty little job.

But this is a pessimistic *Quarterly Essay* and a melancholic one, even if its scathing agnosticism is everywhere touched by a bleak comedy. Watson doesn't believe that Republics – especially the post-modern minimalist one that was envisaged and rejected – are possible or even desirable any more in a world where new fortresses are being erected and the old fear of strangers is being played on in new and surprising ways. And so this pamphlet ends with Watson's version of a modest proposal, a suggestion as shocking to Australian sensibilities as the suggestion that the Irish eat their babies, because it plays on our most fundamental cultural and political fears, our fear of having no haven, no nation worth spitting at. Why don't we just let America swallow us up? Why don't we realise that our true identity is as a cultural footnote to one great empire or another? Why don't we solace our enduring fears of being left in the dark (a prey to all those terrible terrorists and other people we have always been scared of) and throw ourselves into the arms of the big brother who for all his brutality (and for all the family resemblance we cling to, so ambivalently) was always better, brighter, more caring and more beautiful than we could ever be?

But this is a *Quarterly Essay* that plays on all our fundamental fears, including the most terrifying of all that we shall cease to exist because we have never been. It is a black, nearly nihilistic essay, resolutely antipolitical because it comes out of so deep a disdain for politics. It is sustained by the refusal to hope, or to believe that the nation is capable of imagining any future for itself.

It is also, for what it's worth, a sparkling literary performance, an essay almost in a classical mode, full of shifts and slides and attesting to the way a formidable stylist can play with the reader (and with himself) like a cat.

It is a kind of ruminative, laconic monologue Watson has written, a sort of tragicomic soliloquy which takes the form of an anthem for a doomed and dying Australia that is as forlorn and wry as "Waltzing Matilda".

It is shorter than its predecessors and constantly itching towards the condition of epigram. It is not so much an essay that courts or buys into political controversy as one in which the author voids potential positions and vomits them out of his mouth (the biblical injunction reserved for those who were neither hot nor cold). This is an essay which is both very hot and very cold.

It is also a Christmas essay, and Christmas is a good time to publish an essay which is meditative and grave and will provoke the reader as well as beguile her.

It is, believe it or not, a charming essay which will also make the blood run cold.

Peter Craven

RABBIT SYNDROME | *Australia and America*

Don Watson

America is beyond power, it acts as in a dream, as a face of God. Wherever America is, there is freedom, and wherever America is not, madness rules with chains, darkness strangles millions. Beneath her patient bombers, paradise is possible.

John Updike, *Rabbit Redux*

From a certain angle the most terrifying thing in the world is your own life, the fact that it's yours and nobody else's.

John Updike, *Rabbit is Rich*

In 1901 the city fathers of Bendigo, Victoria, purchased for their public gallery an oil by Albert Charles Taylor entitled "Gentlemen, the Queen". Painted in 1894 it portrays, as one would expect, a bevy of whiskery British officers, resplendent in monocles and red uniforms, standing round a dinner table with their glasses raised in the royal toast. It is a portrait of the high Victorian Empire: the spirit is collective and triumphant – if to the jaundiced post-colonial eye also smug, effete and goatish. The ritual formality seems to say, as modern football coaches do, if you keep to the game plan nothing can defeat you. You will have setbacks, the occasional Rorke's Drift, but if you keep to the fundamentals you will end up with an empire whose like has not been seen since time began. The officers immortalised in the painting are profoundly conscious of this.

Around a corner of the same gallery hangs a 1901 portrait by Hugh Ramsay of one "Charles Schneider Esq. Of Cincinnati USA". Mr Schneider is clear-eyed and clean-shaven, impeccably groomed, unambiguously masculine, confident, whole. Ramsay captured in his subject that untrammelled look Americans give the world, as if to say, "I am of the republic. I do not know doubt. I am sufficient." Mr Schneider could only come from the United States. "God has predestinated, mankind expects, great things from our race; and great things we feel in our souls …" Like the men in the first painting, he represents an empire: the American empire which, like the British one, saw itself as blessed by providence and fulfilling nothing less than its "Manifest Destiny". Schneider and the British officers are all in a sense frontiersmen, people on the limits of imperial expansion. But the differences could not be more obvious. It is not just the contrast between Mr Schneider's rugged individualism and the formal collectivity of the British: his "can do" opposed to their "must do". It's a matter of consciousness. The British know they are imperialists and they have uniforms, rituals, a vast literature, a queen, a "natural dogma" to speak for that fact; though his country has recently fought and won an expansionary war with Spain and is making a determined territory-swallowing drive into the Asia-Pacific, though it subscribes to an imperial doctrine and is indeed an imperial power, Mr Schneider knows only that he is an American.

The Americans of Charles Schneider's Gilded Age were less inclined to talk about an American empire than an American marketplace. The distinction has proved a little confusing over the years, as it did for some of its early exemplars. Explaining the idea in 1899, Francis B. Thurber of the United States Export Association succeeded in sounding at once confused and very like a modern corporate boss or politician: "I do not believe in imperialism ... but I do believe in a policy of expansion which will give us the control of some markets which will be a steppingstone to others in a wider zone of influence which such control would enable us to exercise." Thurber's was one voice in a chorus demanding that the United States elbow its way into suitable places for dumping the national surplus, but he shared the widely held view that imperialism, at least on the British model, was un-American. Its being British was one reason for not liking it. The possession of colonies was repellent to the republic. Yet there were economic imperatives and these inevitably became political imperatives, and from the union was born – or reborn – the peculiarly American idea that what was good for American commerce was good for human liberty and happiness, wherever the necessary critical mass of consumers happened to be gathered – in China and Japan, for instance. And what with the way of geopolitics, and the behaviour of natives, it sometimes proved necessary to follow Kipling's advice to take up the white man's burden and actually *impose* a bit of influence in some parts; like Cuba and Puerto Rico and the Philippines and some of those islands out there in the Pacific. Even *annexation* might even be necessary in some cases, and if one truly believed in free commerce (and what true American did not?) one would not flinch from that prospect, especially as each and every means of commercial expansion meant extending the domain of US "National thought" as well. Furthermore, goddamnit, that same course would extend less evil and more progress to the natives of these countries according to the "principles of humanity" on which American commerce rests in the first place. If, in the pursuit of their legitimate interests (surplus dumping, for instance) American citizens or American trade or commerce were injured by some "unjust, cruel and despotic rule", their government would "take a hand in the correction of the evil". But there were to be no songs of empire. It was asserting a country's right to take its produce to market, nothing more and nothing less. It was a *God-given* right, literally, under the doctrine of Manifest Destiny.

That doctrine has endured, though the name and the details have changed: the Truman Doctrine, the Eisenhower Doctrine, the Johnson Doctrine, the Nixon Doctrine and Pax Americana. These were "only extensions of the Monroe Doctrine", I.F. Stone, the radical Washington publicist, insisted in the days of Vietnam. "… [W]e have long been an imperialistic people," he said and it was "poppycock" pretending Vietnam was an exception. Many have marched up to the US Embassy chanting slogans about US imperialism. But inside they wouldn't hear of it. It has been the same for a century and a half. They "plague South America in the name of liberty", Simon Bolivar complained.

In the hundred years since the painting of Schneider and the purchase of "Gentlemen …" Australia has floated between the two worlds of these paintings. Each of them receding and looming according to their interests and our desires. It was always hard to say which one we ought to paddle towards.

These days we are in no doubt about it: we are America's deputy and trusty as they come. Ask not whether this is an honourable destiny and a fitting conclusion to a century of nationhood; it is a *fait accompli*, both sides of politics broadly agree upon it, the question is inadmissible. If we wish, we may attempt to tease out a little of the character of the sheriff; not with the intention of passing judgement on the relationship or on our mighty friend, but with the notion that looking at America might reflect some light on this country and on the options open to us. What is appropriate behaviour in the context of our relationship? We look at America as Gaul — or somewhere more far-flung — might have looked at Rome, as a cat might look at a king. The writer is no expert on American habits or history. He has made only brief visits to America and has never lived there. His knowledge of foreign policy is rudimentary. But for the apparent presumption of his writing this essay he begs to be excused. Like all other Australians he has lived with the Americans all his life. He also knows a few Americans who have lived here for many years and with the best possible will it cannot be said that they know much about Australia. It is true that Alexis de Tocqueville, who is quoted here several times and whose *On Democracy in America* is enjoying a remarkable revival as a source of almost transcendent wisdom on the subject, wrote from the experience of a nine-month whirlwind tour. It is also true that Mark Twain spent much more time in Australia than I have spent on any one journey to America and he concluded that South Australia was a working-man's paradise. My case rests.

2.   And let us always remember that with ourselves, almost for the first time in the history of the earth, national selfishness is unbounded philanthropy; for we can not do a good to America but we give alms to the world.

Henry Melville, *White Jacket*

As children growing up in the 1950s we were not encouraged to like the Americans. They saved Australia in the Coral Sea and we were not to forget it. They were to be preferred to the Russians and Chinese, and any other communists or Asians – that went without saying. We enjoyed most of those Rodgers and Hammerstein musicals. By the age of ten I think I knew the words to most of *Oklahoma* and much of *South Pacific*, along with many songs by Harry Belafonte, Guy Mitchell, Elvis Presley, Bing Crosby and Peggy Lee. Soon after, bumptiously, I took to American jazz. It is unprecedented, surely, but so universal and thoroughgoing in Australian experience that it goes unremarked – almost all the songs of our youth were those of another culture, all the rhythms and beats, all the sentiments. It is hard to say which is the more astonishing – that America filled this basic need almost exclusively, or that America had such a genius for pleasure and invention. When suffering fits of anti-Americanism it is always helpful to try to imagine the world without those songs: no Cole Porter or Irving Berlin or Fats Waller or Gershwin or Kern or Rodgers or Hart. No Billie Holiday, no blues, no rhythm and blues, no Patsy Cline. Just George Formby and Rolf Harris. Or no Frank Capra and Billy Wilder for that matter. Think of the void in our imagining without Monroe or Brando or *Psycho* or *Vertigo*. No Cecil B. de Mille.

In their early teens, my father tells me, he and his brother ran seven miles after milking the cows to see *The Ten Commandments*. That must have been the mid-twenties. Thirty years later we trooped in with him to see the waters part in Technicolor and Cinemascope. The Americans coloured in the world and enlarged it. Britain remained our anchor, but the sea was turning American. We laughed at the Marx Brothers, Danny Kaye and Judy Holliday, liked Cary Grant and Katharine Hepburn, adored Grace Kelly – the princess they longed to have, we thought. We tolerated westerns, mainly I suspect because they made a heroic context for the kind of rural pioneering from which we ourselves were only recently removed. (Heroic but watching Alan Ladd chopping at the tree stump in *Shane* we also laughed.) Certain American faces were irresistible: it is even possible that we hoped our own would evolve into something resembling Gary Cooper's or Gregory Peck's, and that behind the cragginess the same laconic rectitude and sexual magnetism would shine. As for the annihilation of the Indian nations, who were we to protest?

In general we felt at home with the Americans, so long as they were showing their wholesome side. We thought it wise to be friends with them, though it was mainly in the way one is friendly with relations. It was a mantra of one's elders that deep down the Americans envied us our Queen. They would not admit it, of course – being such an unnatural thing, an English-speaking republic, they had to defend it – but you could tell, we reckoned, that they regretted their revolutionary turning. That was why they were so predisposed to boastfulness and rank consumerism – it was compensatory behaviour. Our analysis had something in common with Bob Menzies' observation in the 1930s that any American who has "remotely any English, Scotch or Irish blood ... tells you about it right away". Essentially they were distant cousins, Calvinistic like ourselves, yet even that appeared to be in name only. I seem to remember the family filing out of *Cat on a Hot Tin Roof* well before the end of the first reel. It was impossible to believe that Big Daddy and my father were both Presbyterians. It was unimaginable that we would ever sink to such depths of self-indulgence, such rank confessions. The differences more than the similarities struck us as remarkable, and of all the differences the most disturbing was their dark side.

The B-Grade flicks (not that we knew, but they included classics of film noir) that played in the first half of every program at the country picture theatre where we went had too much shadow and menace. Why would you want to make films about such sleaze? Why dig it up? I would be forever haunted by the image of Gloria Graham with her face wrapped in bandages after Lee Marvin, whose moll she played, threw boiling coffee over her. It was the sort of thing that happened in America, and not just because there was always boiling coffee around. And whisky, for heaven's sake – they drank it like tea. And mumbling narcissists (known as Method actors) with sallow faces and weak chins we did not like; nor films whose themes were juvenile alienation and rebellion and those underground torrents of obsession, horror, lust and violence flowing directly to that everlasting hell over which, it is said, the New England Puritans imagined their lives suspended. If, poor souls, they were condemned by their history to play out forever the unresolved drama of their forebears' twisted imagination, we were sorry but it was not to our taste. The United States had been and remained our saviour, but it did not mean we approved of their Manichean mindset, or enjoyed the oppression of their wealth and ego, or the seeming chaos of their appetites. Even their wholesomeness seemed a little *too* wholesome sometimes: I fancy we suspected it owed less to a love of virtue than an unhealthy awareness of depravity.

More than anything we loathed their war films. You would have thought no one else on the Allied side had fired a shot. Not only did they claim to have won the war single-handed, they changed the context to suit themselves. It was as if they really thought that they had been the only ones to resist the evil, and the only ones who knew what evil was. But of course that is probably the deepest thought in the culture. In *Air Force One*, a recent Hollywood blockbuster directed by a German with his tongue firmly in his cheek, the leader of a terrorist squad (played by the English actor Gary Oldman) takes control of the President's jet and declares he will kill everyone including the President's wife and children unless his demands are met. Oldman delivers a persuasive denunciation of America's role in the ruin of modern Russia. No person of average intelligence could fail to acknowledge that he has at least a reasonable case; but the Americans, especially the President (Harrison Ford), are in no mood to debate – even for a moment. To be American in this world is to be beyond the reach of others' reason – Air Force One, the President, his wife and staff are all of themselves good. Interlopers are vandals, demons, creatures of Evil. And indeed they *are* in this case, but it is still a Monroe Doctrine by another name. "... [D]oes anybody deny the right of this Government," President Cleveland asked rhetorically, "in the interest of humanity, in the interest of the business of this world and the race, to say, 'You must put an end to this condition, or we shall compel you to do so'?" Of course they didn't. After a life-and-death struggle with the terrorist leader, the President (who fights with the warrior-like vigour one expects of a middle-aged American President), assisted by the First Lady, at last gains the upper hand and kicks the evil one into space with the words, "Get off my plane."

The old American war films (like Stephen Spielberg's more recent one, *Saving Private Ryan*) had none of the spirit of *Air Force One*, of course. Those films fulfilled the insatiable American need to make every battle a contest between personifications of Good and Evil absolutely conceived – and one that Good wins narrowly. (Victories over Satan are rare and against the odds, and the thought may lurk in the American mind that alone in the world their country has achieved it.) Everything is reducible to the universal human-interest story. *Schindler's List*, a film about the Holocaust by Stephen Spielberg, is in some mysterious way a human-interest story. On CNN the end of the world will be treated as a human-interest story, and, as with Spielberg's war and Spielberg's Holocaust, watching it happen we will feel that America owns this as well.

We were always very dark on the Americans after we had seen one of their war films. Of course we knew they had been reluctant starters on both occasions, and had only turned on the evil when it turned on them. We didn't have the figures, of course, but they would not have surprised us: the people who claimed to have won the war lost something short of half a million soldiers (and a handful of civilians), many less than died in their civil war. The Russians lost 24 million, the British 3 million, the Chinese 8 million, Poland about 6 million, and in all these cases civilians accounted for anything between a third and two-thirds of the deaths. The Americans provided the materials and munitions, and for their sacrifices – though more for their strength – we were grateful, always, and no less grateful because we knew that they grew richer from that war. But from their films we could only infer that they were boasters and ignoramuses who neither knew the facts of others' histories nor cared to find out. Nothing could provoke them to recognise the sacrifice of others. "It was a good war," says Mrs Smith to Harry Angstrom in John Updike's *Rabbit Run*: "It wasn't like the first. It was ours to win and we won it." They say it to this day. Tom Wolfe was saying it – belligerently – in *Harper's* millennium edition last year. It is less the preposterousness of the claim than the way it confirms that the American mind has bone where in normal people there is space for another's reality. In truth those films seemed more gormless than sinister. They confirmed our view that the Americans had many of the characteristics of children, and that some of the worst things they did were the result of innocence. Yet it still felt like imperialism; an assault not only on common sense and knowledge, but also on our dignity and sovereignty.

British films were different; there was something more truthful and honourable about them. Indeed, reduced to its bare bones, our film criticism came down to the following three categories: true story, based on fact, far-fetched. The British rated highly in the first two, the American product tended to congregate around the last. We also believed, despite much evidence to the contrary, that the Americans lacked a sense of humour, at least one of British standards. They lacked IRONY and, notwithstanding their propensity to spin tales that were far-fetched, took themselves altogether TOO SERIOUSLY. But then the British, who had always written their own war histories as if all Commonwealth troops were "British", withdrew east of Suez and joined up with Europe. What were we to do? Make our own films?

There was one very good reason why we put up with the American and British films – we were embarrassed by our own. And we were right to be. Much else made us cringe, and much has been written about it, but the only point to make here is that we cringed to Britain, not the United States. Our publishing and literary taste was largely determined in Britain, our graduates studied in British universities, our intellectual and creative talents expatriated themselves to Britain, we continued to think of ourselves as essentially British and our upper and educated classes faithfully imitated theirs. In the 1950s when the Australian architect Robin Boyd complained bitterly about the excruciating "Cockneyesque whine" of the Australian accent, it was "visiting Englishmen" he was worried about displeasing, and he was not suggesting an Americanesque accent instead.

Culturally speaking, Britain, not the United States, was our Mecca and our measure. Even as we eagerly joined with the US in the Vietnam conflict, saw the American share in investment and control of our industries creep up on the British, and succumbed to American popular culture, it was to Britain that we looked for culture and meaning. Indeed we looked there as a way of balancing the American influence. For some of the influential middle class – even in my own non-middle class childhood environment – the British connection was the best prophylactic in an increasingly American world. It even enabled us to look down on the Americans for being the philistines they were. It was not just a matter of their economic imperialism. It was a cultural position. So deep did this belief run that not only the Left but also our liberal intellectuals and literati (gathered for instance round the otherwise noble journal *Meanjin*) were much more often to be heard damning Washington and Disneyland than Moscow and the Gulag. So unremitting was their loathing of American films, television and advertising and the popular culture they imagined it reflected, that it seems very likely they also loathed Americans.

Of course we did not give up without a fight. We got our own TV industry going and grafted it on the two great imported streams. From time to time we made a great fuss about the local cultural product, even when it sent us up mercilessly – indeed this seemed to be the way we liked it. We found all sorts of ways to pretend we were upright and firmly on our own two feet, but in truth we bent over the barrel and were willing to bend further as occasion demanded. The reality of our actual position being fairly loathsome, such advertisements as we wrote for ourselves were essentially disguises. As it had been with the British, so it became with the Americans: the culture was a carapace to hide the truth from ourselves and others. We were as shrill and brash as the Americans sometimes, though not with their naïveté: with us it was the opposite, a spirit corrupted by the weakness of our position in the world and our dependence on powerful friends. Lurking behind our self-confidence was anxiety and shame.

Unable to conceive of any independent strategy in Asia after the British withdrawal, we egged on the Americans in Vietnam and sent the army in to fight for them, as "mercenaries" as one veteran recently said. We had no say in the conduct of the war, and appeared not to want any. Because the Americans were conscripting their young men for the war, we conscripted ours – as many as we could afford to train, through a ballot that was unconscionable but convenient. While Australian soldiers fought in Vietnam, at home other Australians demonstrated against the war. *We* knew the Americans were imperialists even if the Americans did not.

Never had there been less reason to believe in communism, but anti-Americanism managed to turns hordes of bright young people into Marxists, Leninists, Maoists, Trotskyists and anarchists – revolutionaries. America being multitudinous and market-supple, Americans provided most of the music for the revolution. And the clothing, hair and lifestyles, heroes, role models, buzz-words, artwork, poetry, novels, journalism and comic books. Mao and Ho Chi Minh somehow became anti-authoritarian figures, to be admired at the same time as one read Ken Kesey and lived like the Merry Pranksters. What great days they were. Add marijuana, LSD and sexual liberation, and the mind of the average opponent of American imperialism had something of the atmosphere of a Saigon bar.

3.   The big Mouseketeer has appeared, Jimmie, a grown man who wears circular black ears. Rabbit watches him attentively; he respects him. He expects to learn something from him helpful in his own line of work, which is demonstrating a kitchen gadget in several five-and-dime stores around Brewer … Jimmy sets aside his smile and guitar and says straight out through the glass "Know Thyself, a wise old Greek once said. Know thyself. Now what does this mean, boys and girls?"

John Updike, *Rabbit Run*

John Updike's Rabbit quartet is on one reading a denunciation of American society as merciless and foetid as anything written about Rome or Babylon. It began in 1960 with *Rabbit Run*. Harry "Rabbit" Angstrom, high-school basketball hero, flees one night from his pregnant "poor dumb mutt" of a wife, Janice, his two-year-old son and their home in Brewer, Pennsylvania. He drives the dreadful highways to West Virginia; from nowhere to nowhere. But he can't quite do it, so he goes back; back to Brewer, and his old basketball coach, the egregious Tothero who introduces him to the prostitute Ruth. Ruth turns out to be just about the only person of any moral density in the whole saga (unless it is Thelma, an unloved friend's wife who loves Harry, who is dying of lupus, whom he sodomises on request, of whom he says to her husband at her funeral, "She was a fantastic lay.") Alas, Rabbit leaves Ruth, rising from her bed in the middle of the night when the minister (with whom he regularly plays golf) rings to tell him that Janice is in labour. Fourteen years later Janice leaves Harry for a Greek car salesman, and Harry sets up house with their son, Nelson, and an eighteen-year-old teenage junkie whose body he shares with Skeeter, a messianic Negro. He runs the gamut of seventies decadence and Reaganite reaction. He reads, almost exclusively, *Consumer Reports*, and its verdicts form the staple of his conversation. He is a man of almost incredible crassness. His sexual obsession is inexhaustible and highly tuned. Nothing else comes close to exercising his imagination like the merest suggestion of nipples or pussy. He stops thinking of female possibility only when survival instincts compel some other thought – to sell a Toyota, watch television, eat salted peanuts or improve his golf swing. (Rabbit has a little in common with Homer Simpson.) Or to indulge in some second-hand patriotism – Pop, if you like, to the Mom of his pudenda fantasies. Rabbit is a Christian, Updike makes a point of telling us early in the first book.

But we get the feeling that Rabbit has some greatness in him. His instincts are sure, even if his thinking is not. Life and death might frighten him, but no earthly being does. His love of the female body, while obsessive, is unrestrained and marvellous in the detail of observation. He glories in it. From these reflections and others about Toyota Corollas and salted peanuts we are left in no doubt that he is both sentient and conscious. And Rabbit has an occasional intimation about death and the human condition that defies his platitudinous myopia and brainlessness and puts him well clear of the lower primates. Just now it is startling to discover in the mind of the one character the observation that "all in all", America just has to be the "happiest … country the world has ever seen", and the thought he has at the start of the final volume that the plane arriving with his hopeless son on board portends his own demise. Open-heart surgery and angioplasty can't save Rabbit: he eats himself to death, dying on a suburban basketball court in his mid-fifties, trying to recapture youth's glories 40 pounds above a healthy weight. He could go no other way, unless it was on the golf course, or in the middle of that other addiction of the American male, a blow job.

The Rabbit books may be read in various ways – for example, as a ruthless dissection of the male psyche (Rabbit is outrageous but never less than familiar); as a satire on the human condition or modern American life; as an unsentimental but ultimately forgiving domestic portrait; as an elegy for the soul of America, torn between God and Nature, a sort of visceral proof that American commerce was, as Perry Miller said, "conceived in the bed of religion". Updike steps into the "woeful putrefaction" the old Puritan preachers saw at the centre of New England life, but not to judge as they did, only to describe or to laugh or to join the general melancholy. He does not need to judge, it is enough that he sees. He sees the hollowness at the centre, the door closed to possibility. "Your life has no reflective content," Jill, Rabbit's eighteen-year-old lay, tells him. "It's all instinct and when your instinct lets you down, you have nothing to trust. That's what makes you cynical. Cynicism is tired pragmatism. Pragmatism suited a certain moment here, the frontier moment, it did the work very wastefully and ruthlessly but it did it." But it's no longer useful. "You carry an old God with you, and an angry old patriotism," she says. Jill burns to death in Rabbit's house while he stands outside and watches with his disintegrating twelve-year-old.

Ruth, the abandoned lover, is more direct – she calls him "Mr Death himself. You're not just nothing, you're worse than nothing." So Rabbit, "a typical good-hearted, imperialist racist", his body a decaying vessel poisoned by fast food and wasted potential, his imagination dimmed by prejudice and television, running on ignorance and fear, smears with shit those few things which are pure, Ruth says, and echoes the emptiness Updike sees at the core of America.

Naturally Rabbit has been equated with Uncle Sam himself. He is coarse, philistine and provincial; he is alienated from the land, religion and history, from his children, his imagination and his potential. Like a real rabbit he lives by his appetites for sex and food, and like a real American he tries to fill the remaining space with golf, daiquiris and dreams of a house with a sunken living room: the small objects to which, if the pursuit of happiness is to mean anything and a democracy is to work, the soul clings. "One does not see anything until one sees its beauty," Oscar Wilde said. Poor Rabbit sees beauty only in ass or a three-pointer — and money which he associates with ass in any case. He reunites with his wife for the convenience of her father's money and a job at his Toyota agency. Taking advantage of a surge in gold prices after the Russian invasion of Afghanistan, he buys bullion, spreads it on the matrimonial bed and he and the mutt rut like rabbits in it. It's the unex-amined life — worse the unimagined life — taken to its highest point. So it was inevitable that the Rabbit quartet would be called "a powerful critique of America".

It is not, of course, a critique we have to accept, any more than we are obliged to take George W. Bush as representative of the American mind. The truth could lie anywhere between the President and Gore Vidal and other perennially disenchanted American souls. Foreign critics of the United States should not kid themselves: no scorn of theirs will match what Americans say about themselves. "If you find so much that is unworthy of reverence in the United States, then why do you live here?" H.L. Mencken asked himself. "Why do men go to zoos?" he replied.

Nowhere else are the words "free" and "freedom" so pervasive. Their anthem proclaims the land of the free, and no patriotic American speech fails to mention it. And in many ways, no doubt, it is a remarkably free country. Australians make much less of the idea, taking it more for granted, perhaps because Britain for so long seemed to guarantee it. The absence of the word from our public rhetoric and popular writing, relative to America at least, may also be due in part to a first half-century when a significant proportion of the population was *not* free. Upon their emancipation, convicts in Australia calculated that it was not in their interests to draw attention to the past by singing songs of freedom, unlike black Americans who were in no position to hide the fact that they had once been slaves. Like the *Star Spangled Banner, Advance Australia Fair* declares that we are free, but the observation is granted no more status than the one in the next line that the country is an island. The Americans, of course, are less "girt by sea", but, even if they were girt entirely, it is doubtful they would feel constrained to say so in their national anthem.

It is without doubt the strangest country when it comes to politics. For all their unequivocal professions of love, the idea of freedom seems to produce in Americans a good deal of fear. In the citadel of freedom, the child of the enlightenment, the word "liberal" now carries the same meaning as its opposite. Desperate to avoid branding, candidates for office weave and dart and burrow in all directions, for to be identified as a "liberal" today is rather like being tagged "communist" a generation ago. In 1996 Lewis Lapham, the liberal editor of *Harper's*, noted the publication of a book by Robert H. Bork, a Yale Law Professor nominated by Ronald Reagan for the Supreme Court and in 1996 a regular guest on the major American talk shows. The book, called *Slouching towards Gomorrah,* was a jeremiad from one who, in his own words, "detests modern liberalism and all its works". For modern liberalism, read multiculturalists, radical feminists, homosexual activists, black extremists, intellectual "nihilists" and various other categories of people consumed by hatred and "contempt for American society". This diatribe sounds familiar to our own ears, of course, accustomed as they now are to the abuse of "élites", special interest groups, black armband historians, pushy blacks and chattering classes. But it is much more pungent in its American context, where it comes with slavering endorsements from the Christian Coalition and various influential right-wingers. *Slouching towards Gomorrah* quickly hit the best-seller lists. Lapham noted its resemblance to medieval millenarian tracts, with its lists of modern "liberals" as the equivalents of tenth-century associates of Satan. Most remarkable was Bork's wish to jettison the enlightenment in which the republic was created and recreate the United States as a Puritan theocracy.

The book was published in the same week as the Taliban seized control of most of Afghanistan, an irony that Lapham did not fail to note. He doubted if the Taliban had read Bork, yet even without him, "they seemed to know how to go about the great task of putting an end to the nonsense of liberty and equality."

We need not accept such acerbic views of America. We can agree with any of the more favourable assessments: that it is the best society yet achieved in an imperfect world, through to the one revived in recent times casting America as the repository of Good in the war against Evil — from Homer Simpson to Ned Flanders next door if you will. Of course, just the other day those now most fervently casting it as Good were the ones saying it was sunk in Evil, and for the same people the city of the twin towers was the proof of it. New York was Gomorrah on the Hudson. But who are we to talk if American politics is full of contradictions? We vilify people fleeing from the tyranny we are fighting. Whether we think America is essentially good or positively bad does not matter in the end: it is very likely both – it contains multitudes, as Walt Whitman said of himself. What matters is that Australia exhibits negative traits of culture and personality very like those we and others see exhibited in the United States.

Perhaps Rabbit is a metaphor that Updike never intended: a distant metaphor for the soul of Australia, the country which, like Rabbit, recoils in fear from the insight that its life is its own and no one else's, and changes the angle to accommodate its fear. The country that tries but cannot leave the safety of an unsatisfying union (not the British, nor the Americans) and abandons anything more challenging even when it knows that fulfilment lies there. Whose imagination works only in fits and starts, flutters into life under the impulse of certain stimuli and then settles back into the familiar and second-hand. That, if recent indications can be trusted, is losing the capacity that Rabbit wonders at in women – the "strange way they have … of really caring about somebody beyond themselves". The country that declares itself the luckiest and best on earth and listens avidly to shock jocks abusing anyone who suggests otherwise while all the time telling us how bad it is; whose appetite for crap is bottomless; that talks high principles but values pragmatism and practices unqualified self-interest; substitutes platitudes for wisdom; suffers the same Protestant curse but without the fires of hell to warm it. That seeks shelter beneath those American bombers and just now shows every sign that it will find its definition there: huddling rabbit-like, never venturing too far from the burrow.

Whether this is consequent on prolonged exposure to the United States, or to our ranking as eager ally and client state, is difficult to say. Our flaws may be endemic, their likeness to Rabbit Angstrom's mere coincidence. But it is too much of a coincidence, surely, and too much bad luck that we should get more of the flaws and less of the strengths. Would that we had an Updike; or a Melville; or a Mark Twain. Has anyone documented the Australian condition as they have the American? Is the Australian condition sufficient to such talents, or even capable of producing them? Would that we had the Americans' confidence. A small portion of their inventiveness. Just one of their best universities or research institutes. Two of their best five hundred companies. Some of their instinct for philanthropy. Some of their genius. If just five or ten per cent of their immigrants had chosen Australia instead. Would that we had been so open and so civilised. Note that we are not asking for their rivers and plains, or any other natural advantages – just small things, but reflections of a spirit that they have abundantly and we, along with most other countries, seem to lack.

And, yes, they did win the war – at least it could not have been won without them. And with the Marshall Plan they saved Western Europe after it. Saved it? They made it. And they did save Australia. Just as they saved millions in accordance with the sentiment expressed on the Statue of Liberty. They have been a mighty force for freedom. Flawed, contradictory, murderous, outrageous; yet what empire in history was less malevolent? Which one did more good works? And imagine the world without Louis Armstrong.

And if none of this persuades you, resort to the relativities – think of Eastern Europe, North Korea as opposed to the South. A visit to the border north of Seoul in the early nineties was instructive: before reaching it one received instruction from a Strangelovian American officer in terms that were a poor parody of Kubrick's film. "Do not taunt or by any gesture even inadvertent provoke the communist soldiers on the other side of the parallel. Remember you are a TARGET." It would be hilarious if his demeanour had not been *comparatively* sane and his words essentially true. On the other side lunatic propaganda blared from loudspeakers, benighted soldiers strutted around trying to affect, and quite possibly feeling, the belligerence of true communists towards the capitalist enemy. If our side feels a bit like Hollywood, on the other side lie real madness, real ignorance and, one cannot help sensing, real evil. Whatever we might say about the Americans we need never be in any doubt, not so far anyway, that it is both wise and proper to be on their side in the greater swim of things.

4. "Maximum fine in 1829 for teaching an African-American living in Georgia to read or write – $500."

"Ratio [in 2000] of the number of pupils per teacher in Michigan's schools to the number of inmates per guard in its prisons: 18:5."

Harper's Index, Fall 2001

"Our Government makes no sense unless it is founded on a deeply held religious faith, and I don't care what it is."

Dwight Eisenhower

The question is, however, what is the wise and proper way to be on their side? It might help to begin by recognising how little we have in common with them, how unalike we are, what distant cousins. Occasionally there have been signs of real affinity between our leaders. But whatever genuine affections existed between Holt and Johnson, the relationship between the two countries concerned little more than the Vietnam War and it was all one way. Hawke and George Bush had something going between them: but beyond the Gulf War, what sustained it? Perhaps uniquely, Keating and Clinton found common ground on a raft of issues and a genuine liking for each other. Their first meeting in Washington was remarkable not only for the obvious warmth between them, but because it was based on a shared policy vision, both international and domestic. They agreed broadly on health and education policy, on political strategies for social democratic parties, on trade liberalisation and the extension of APEC. It was a meeting of new Democrat and Labor minds at which Australia actually brought to the table something of weight for both sides. Doubtless my bias is showing, but it had rarely if ever been like this before, and it has certainly not been like it since.

Much responsibility for the failure attaches to Australian leaders without enough ideas, gumption or force of personality to impress this country's interests or philosophy upon the leadership of the most powerful nation on earth. How could APEC and Australia's role in it be allowed to slide as it has in the past five years? No doubt it got harder with Clinton later in his Presidency, and harder still with George W. Bush; but just as surely the will to keep the Americans engaged with what we thought, especially what we thought about the region, dramatically faded, as if it had wilted in the heat of the shining light. Perhaps the words and gestures were not intended to convey so plainly our change of heart, our mental baulk at the regional challenge; perhaps this was *exactly* what was intended by them. It really doesn't matter: you only have to think like a deputy to look like a deputy, and look like a deputy long enough and one day they'll pin a badge on you and tell you to shut up and do as you're told. Too late then to discover your independence if the sheriff asks for something that it is not in your interests or nature to give. Too late to insist that you represent more than the sheriff's interests. Too late if you raise your gaze one day and see something weird or sinister lurking in the sheriff's eyes.

The Americans are different. Or should we say that we are? There are the obvious measures. We do not hang, fatally inject, gas, electrocute or shoot people found guilty of murder. The Americans do it to hundreds every year. Were we to engage in capital punishment, it is unlikely we would long entertain the idea that the general public had a right or a need to *witness* executions. The Americans take the idea very seriously. It is probably true that if the matter were to be determined by a popular vote, capital punishment would be reinstated in most if not all the States of Australia.

But we do not determine it this way. There is no great clamour to execute criminals, and were there to be, an even greater clamour would oppose it. We read of Americans executing their fellow citizens, hear otherwise enlightened Americans supporting the procedure; see images on television of the devices they employ, the prisoner walking to the chair or table; and some of us think these people are not like us, *fundamentally*. There's something cruel and ghoulish about them. They missed a stage in the progress of western civilisation. If it happens in China, it does not surprise: we don't expect the Chinese to be like us. We don't expect it of some European countries, yet the abolition of capital punishment is a condition of membership of the European Union. We tend to assume the Americans are progressing on the same intellectual and moral plane; and then we hear on the TV that sage Gary Cooper lookalike, Executive Assistant District Attorney Jack McCoy of *Law and Order*, urging the death penalty for some poor sod avarice or anger got the better of. Bill Clinton also thinks (or has been known to feign to think) capital punishment is an essential ingredient of a criminal justice system. He agrees with us about a public health system and a public education system and human rights and free trade in the Asia-Pacific; and he is also so ardent (and cynical) an executioner we read that in pursuit of popular approval, as Governor of Arkansas, he went out of his way to be in his home State on the day a long-time inhabitant of death row, who had suffered brain damage, was put to death. This is so gross that it reminds us of (though it bears no comparison to) Stalin playing cat and mouse with his victims or Hitler repeatedly watching films of participants in the 1944 "Officers' Plot" being executed. It reminds us of every tyrant and debauchee who never learned reason or restraint. And the present incumbent? We read that during his term as Governor of Texas more than a hundred people were executed.

Then there are the guns. Charlton Heston, another one of the granite-faced Americans of the fifties, Moses in the Technicolor *Ten Commandments*, turns out to be a paranoid macho screwball. They are *mad* about guns, as mad as any people on earth about them. And there is not just the violence, there's the accompanying theme of revenge that runs through the movie culture. As if they still take the Old Testament literally. We live for the most part with the comforting belief – so comforting we are barely conscious of it – that they are a lot like us, these Americans we see on TV and in the movies and read about in the papers so much we think we know them as well as we know ourselves. They're a bit whacky, of course (so are Rex Hunt and Bob Hawke in their ways), but on the whole they are clever and civilised. Then suddenly a news item jolts us, or some scrap of information from the Internet or *Harper's* Index, and for a moment they seem to have more in common with an Albanian blood cult than with our own civilisation. Very often the news coming out of America suggests that the theocracy to which Robert H. Bork wants to return never went away.

It's not a theocracy, of course; and religion, though it wields an unusual influence, is not the nub of it. It's the history of the place – English, French and Spanish, the whole caboodle. Not just the history but what they have made of it. It is also the Mohawk, Mohicans, Cherokee, Nez Perce, Comanches, Apaches and Sioux. There was war of a kind on the Australian frontier. There was bloodshed and cruelty, but it did not sear itself into the founding myths and the national psyche like two centuries of Indian wars did in America. Indeed the Indian wars got themselves more thoroughly into Australian psyches than any conflict with the

Aborigines did. For those of us who as children read *Tom Sawyer*, *The Last of the Mohicans* and *Ned in the Woods*, terror took an American shape in our brains long before we saw John Wayne hunting Natalie Wood and the Indians out west in *The Searchers*.

The frontier in Australian history was a very different thing. Russell Ward famously argued that unlike America, where the spirit that emerged was individualistic, the conditions of the Australian frontier produced mateship, unions, a collectivist ethos. In fact the term itself was scarcely used – a "frontier" was per se American and it meant a place of violence. We were raised to believe that the Aborigines hardly put up a fight and therefore little force was needed to remove them. It was a kind of anti-myth, a story without heroes or villains, save Daisy Bates, a missionary who might have been both, a story without influence on the national character. The whole episode of settlement came to us as essentially passive and lacking in drama. As children we were not entirely quarantined from the cruelty inflicted upon Aboriginal Australians, nor from moral judgement; but what had been swept under the carpet was left there. It was when a new generation of scholars began sweeping it into view that a new generation of thought police stepped in and denounced "black arm-band" history – meaning immoderate, bad, even unpatriotic history. The Americans romanticised their frontier wars, made myths from them, as usual turned their Manichean lenses on them, but they did not on the whole adopt this odious anti-intellectualism – it was a long while ago, why dig up the past? Even Hollywood, as eventually it does in most things, took a revisionist view and the frontier it portrays, even in its most stylised and parodic products, has vastly more truth and reality about it than anything the Australian film industry has produced. Even that old redneck John Ford in the end made amends to the Indians with *Cheyenne Autumn*.

In Australia, for all the efforts of Henry Reynolds (and of his opponents, for that matter), the national mind has never been so numb to the reality and the meaning of the frontier – or so uninterested. We wallow in comforting platitudes enlivened recently by occasional spats about the numbers killed in massacres. The effect of these arguments is first to polarise our history along the same ideological lines as divide our politics, and second to extinguish interest in the subject. These days some Australians are determined to believe that very few Aborigines were killed, while perhaps as many (with more credibility, I would maintain) are just as set on a great number. Meanwhile, a third, much larger complement grows increasingly conscientious in not giving a damn. Far from enlightening us or even making us think or feel something about these seminal events, the debate over the last few years has ground into confusion and such comforting platitudes from the highest reaches of power as, "I don't think Australians want to dwell on all the bad things." And those that do want to dwell on them, or escape such noxious pap, if they wish may turn to the latest book about Ned Kelly, the only nineteenth-century Australian still more than half-alive in the public imagination.

Americans may turn to Cormac McCarthy or Larry McMurtry; or, for instance, to any one of several film treatments of Jesse James and Billy the Kid. When they do they find psychologically complex, historically imaginative, subtle, savage, uncompromising takes on their history that Australians ought to envy. One of Hollywood's great gifts to the world was imagined history. Hollywood understood that the past was a field to be cultivated by interpretation, and had the studios been asked they might have agreed with Carlyle that the history of the world was but the biography of great men. The results have been often hilariously and nauseatingly bad, but they have also given Americans at the very least an impression of the past, even an engagement with it, relatively free of the constraints of "period". Look at the various screen takes on Billy the Kid; from Arthur Penn's to Marlon Brando's to Sam Peckinpah's to Gore Vidal's. It has to be healthy for a country to turn its heroes and villains upside down and shake them, to see what secrets they hold. Here, where fact-grubbing has always been at war with the imagination, notwithstanding Sydney Nolan's Kelly series of paintings, we have been less successful at creating a vigorous and imaginative relationship with our history.

It is not just their history but what they have made of it that sets America apart. Compare with the notion of black armband history the portrait of the Old West in decay in *The Wild Bunch*. *The Wild Bunch* celebrates the "bad things". It mourns their passing, not the "innocence" they destroy. In this way it is a very good history lesson of a particular kind. No doubt there are people who "do not want to dwell on the bad things in the past", but that does not mean they should not be made to. If "most Australians" or the "great majority of Australians" do not want to dwell on them, it may be because not enough bad things have been put in front of them. Perhaps that's why, when they see a real live bad thing, like a sinking boat loaded with refugees, they recoil in fear. Perhaps they need a Cormac McCarthy to write about the bad things, to show them that history confronted raw and unexpurgated yields dividends of poetry and awareness, and without fatal damage to a nation's cohesion or psyche. Or perhaps they need Comanches, "a legion of horribles ... gaudy and grotesque with daubings like a company of mounted clowns, death hilarious, all howling in a barbarous tongue riding down upon them like a horde from hell …"

When the Frenchman de Tocqueville visited the United States in the 1830s, the "religious atmosphere of the country" was the first thing that struck him. Not everyone agreed; many, including Emerson, thought religion was in decline and running shallower than before. But it ran infinitely deeper in America than it did in Australia, and in very different ways. Pious and orderly minds, when they surveyed Australia in the 1830s, perceived a worrying absence of religious observance. To this they ascribed most of the moral shortcomings of the people. Among other remedies the abolition of the convict system and the importation of upright single women were suggested. Although the colonial churches were very busy, and the now abandoned, crumbling or depleted churches of Australian town and country still speak for this activity, the ministers wondered even then if religion amounted to much in the parishioners' hearts. "Practical paganism" and its genteel relation "moral enlightenment" prevailed and really they always have. Nothing in Australia prompted the rise of Mormons and Millerites and those countless other sects whose descendants are still at work on modern American television and in modern American politics 160 years later. There was no spontaneous "awakening" of the kind that gripped the American commercial classes in 1858, bringing them together in prayer and persuading all but the most cynical that God and commerce could be mixed. We Australians can add "under God" to a constitutional preamble, and even begin to use the name as freely as it is used in American public discourse, but that will not give us a "religious mind". Few Australians will ever believe their country was "formed by God" as Americans believe of the republic. We will not unite in prayer. And it is difficult to foresee a day when our head of state, seemingly programmed to play out the old Puritan drama once again, confesses to a breakfast prayer meeting of leading clergy that he is liar and a fornicator and begs the forgiveness of the Lord and the nation.

In modern America no political leader can afford not to believe in God as defined by Christianity, for the very good reason that an extraordinary preponderance of the voting population does. Surveys consistently reveal that well over half of Americans believe in heaven and hell. By contrast, less than half agree with the basic proposition of evolution that human beings developed from earlier animal species; and it is possible that one of the people to disagree with this proposition is George W. Bush. The President favours the teaching of both Darwinism and Creationism in schools.

In Australia the decline of traditional religion did not cause so much thrashing about and there were far fewer visitations. No evangelical movement offered a serious challenge. The Protestant and Catholic churches staged their sectarian battles within the familiar guidelines. They vigorously exercised what political influence they could, but rarely broached the lines separating church and state. No one could speak credibly of theocracy. Nietzsche's announcement that God was dead met with the same general equanimity. Alfred Deakin and a little late nineteenth-century theosophy aside, they were less inclined to imparadise their hearts than their hearths: they put their faith in gradual socialism and topped it up with beer, irony and racism. With religion as with the marketplace, Australians did not rush after the main chance so fervently. That's how Americans seemed to us when we were growing up – too much public soul-searching and emoting, too obviously the salesmen of the world, too inclined to do things to excess. There were certain boundaries they seemed not to recognise.

This country was born of a very different union and soldered together not in a fiery furnace but through a protracted series of lawyers' meetings. Its originating documents are entirely without poetry or inspiration, or even an overriding principle; the principles, indeed, are underriding. A fondness for freedom does not need to be spelt out. We are British. Life, liberty and the pursuit of happiness – ditto. The Australian constitution is a statute of the British parliament, creating under the crown of the United Kingdom a Commonwealth, the six colonies as States, and a common market. The guarantees of liberties numbered two: religious tolerance, but only under the Commonwealth and not the States; and freedom from discrimination, but only for residents of one State when in another. Few contemporary Australians know anything about their constitution and fewer still could say which principles it takes for granted. This may be no bad thing, of course. It helps to keep the gap between rhetoric and reality within manageable limits. We are spared much overblown oratory and this helps keep hypocrisy to a manageable level.

Even fewer traces of high purpose attended the foundation of colonial Australia. It was no flight from tyranny to Paradise, try as some officers might to give it a Miltonic dimension and others to detect the hand of Providence. The colony was born purebred British, an outhouse of the old country consequent upon the Americans defeating her in the War of Independence. Several of the early officials of New South Wales, including governors, had fought against the American revolutionaries.

Some thought "American" when they thought "revolutionary" or "republican" or "loud upstart". These men ran a prison. Not a free settlement, a place like pre-revolutionary America where a host of political ideas noisily competed, nor a religious refuge; but a place of punishment and, for some time, religious persecution: a place whose gentry were determined to establish an outrageously privileged land-owning aristocracy, and by 1850 had gone a long way towards achieving their ambition. If what happens in infancy has anything to do with it, the Americans are not our natural allies but much more like our enemies. Twenty-five years after the foundation of the colony, before the settlers had found their way so much as a hundred miles west, before they had seen what the continent looked like, the Americans were waging another war against the British.

The French stayed anchored outside the heads while the Union Jack was raised in Sydney Cove; in America they had a large slice of the continent and much influence on American political philosophy and on American strategic thinking. The Americans also had Spain to deal with. The United States began life as a multicultural society. They had more than two centuries of slavery, from which white Americans grew fat, and a civil war that saved the union and emancipated the slaves at the cost of more than half a million lives. But such were the racial horrors that followed, some wondered if black Americans weren't better off before emancipation; and the robber baron capitalism of Gould, Morgan and the Rockefellers that "dethroned God and set up a shekel in His place" (in Mark Twain's words) made some of America's better souls look back to antebellum America as a serene and just age.

But in case we should get on our high horse, it is also true that Teddy Roosevelt, self-styled hero of the "emotional classes" in their war with

"Economic Man", welcomed a Negro to the White House and appointed a Jew to his Cabinet. At that time Australia's founders were drafting the legislative expression of White Australia.

A recitation of these generally well-known facts is only useful to remind us how different we are; how strangely insignificant and unformed compared to the American experience of wars, awakenings and contendings. There is some kind of measure to be found in the faces of Sherman and Grant, literate, brutal soldier-statesmen of the republic. You don't see those kinds of faces among the fathers of Australian federation. Explorers make another useful comparison. Burke and Wills, Giles, Warburton, Sturt and Stuart found a dead heart in the centre of the continent and the further west they went the worse it got. Their experience gave the country legends whose main themes were irony and fatalism, hard-luck stories. Traversing the land from east to west Lewis and Clark found majesty and riches beyond measure and gave Americans yet more reason to glow with confidence and believe that they were blessed.

Even by the end of the nineteenth century the Americans did not *need* the rest of the world, beyond the purposes of commerce. The United States *was* the world; all a man like Charles Schneider of Cincinnati needed to know, or a boy like Huck Finn needed to discover. George W. Bush might look and sound to us like the dimwit he probably is, but Americans have not cared about how they looked in the world since Jefferson went to Paris. It's why so often when you meet them overseas or hear them talking, you can't help but feel that in the American mind the rest of the world exists as something extraneous to real life.

Turn-of-the-century immigration to America is a mirror image of the same phenomenon. Why should America take on the sensibilities of the rest of the world when the rest of the world wanted to be American? The millions of people who rolled through Ellis Island in the last decade of the old century and the first decades of the new did not come as part of a plan for a multicultural society. They were simply swallowed up by forces more powerful than xenophobia, prejudice, eugenics or any petty human motive for exclusion. They delivered to the United States unstoppable energy, mass, genius, character, hardship, cheap labour, another vast chapter in the American story. The lesson of immigration – through Ellis Island or Station Pier (or Christmas Island) – is always courage. It takes courage for the immigrants to come. It takes courage to take them in. And countries that take them gain courage from doing so.

America's proximity to Europe obviously gave it a great advantage over Australia in the contest for migrants. So too, perhaps, the fact that one destination was a flourishing republic and the other a British colony constructed from a gaol. No person in his right mind would choose a gaol over a republic; just as no one in possession of the facts would choose a British ship over an American. The republic also had the advantage of attracting people from all corners of Europe, including the British Isles; people who, when they arrived, were less inclined than British migrants to Australia to think their stay was temporary or a home away from home. Is it possible that American immigrants more decisively cut the painter with home and were quicker to become American citizens and patriots? For the first hundred and fifty years of Australia's existence the effort was always at least partly to merge Australia's culture, economy, political structure and strategic interest with Britain's. As late as the 1930s R.G. Menzies was putting the case in London. Did Britain feel, he asked his hosts: "… that its sons and brothers, one might almost say its sons and lovers, in Australia, are its own flesh and blood, or does it regard them as 'remittance men'?" The answer, which Menzies said would determine our mutual relations, "not merely for the next five years, but for the next five hundred years", is much less interesting than the question. Menzies was – at this stage of his life at least – tending to obsessiveness about blood. "Also we will make promise so long as the blood endures ..." he wrote on the bottom of one of his speeches. He imagined that the "sixty million people who ought to be in Australia tomorrow" could be at once the answer to Britain's social ills and the key to Australia playing "the part that we ought to play in the future of the British race". It was a theme he returned to repeatedly – Australia was like a son grown to adulthood, and seeking now to play a useful part in the British family. It was not a mercantile relationship but a blood relationship. He could not imagine any surer source of strength than this Britishness, this feeling that "my strength is yours".

There was Menzies' British blend and there was America's hybrid energy. No one can safely say which was the more valuable boatload, but a survey of, say, Australia's most successful post-war entrepreneurs, does suggest that it was not only the tyranny of distance that cost Australia the sort of vigour America enjoyed, but also our colonial status for the first century and our colonial mentality for much of the second.

Great oratory and high principle have always ridden shotgun on American self-interest. The American republic grew with God, the Constitution and the Declaration of Independence to guide it (and, after the Civil War, Lincoln's Gettysburg address). The Australian colonies, if any single guiding light can be discerned at all, trekked manfully towards a "New Britannia in another world". During the Civil War, Her Majesty declared a position of strict neutrality and Australian colonial governments naturally followed suit. Nevertheless, when the confederate raider *Shenendoah* turned up in Port Phillip to land prisoners and take on crew, thousands of citizens went down to the water's edge and cheered her sailors. And a squad of the local élite took the ship's captain and his officers to the Melbourne Club and cheered them too. It is by no means certain that either show of enthusiasm indicated support for the rebel cause over the union, or even approval of the *Shenendoah*'s notorious exploits in the Pacific. (By the end of the war she had plundered or destroyed thirty-six ships.) It was probably enough that she was American.

It was generally our way with the Americans. Twenty-five years earlier Charles Wilkes and two ships from the United States Exploring Expedition, a vast scientific-cum-imperialistic enterprise surveying the Pacific, slipped into Sydney Harbour. Wilkes told his hosts how easily he might have ransacked the place, so poor were its defences. The colonial gentry of New South Wales were only too pleased to show them around. When the US Navy, known as the Great White Fleet, arrived in 1908, Sydney crowds were positively jubilant. We might find them strange and not have a clue what stratagem or interest lay behind their occasional appearances, and we would deny that our response should be taken as admiration or sympathy for the republican course they had taken, but we loved to see them. No doubt it had much to do with our isolation and the comfort of seeing powerful English-speaking white men in this part of the world. But perhaps it was also rather like the way we found their music irresistible, the absence of inhibition, the love of display, their unembarrassed attitude to wealth, the way Fred Astaire and Judy Garland make you feel when they sing "We'll Walk down the Avenue". It is possible that somewhere in our minds we saw in these Americans the people we might have been.

By the time the Australian colonies federated, the United States was a century-old republic and a burgeoning imperial power. While Australians scratched together a constitution in the midst of a drought, a rabbit plague, an economic depression and a British war in South Africa, the Americans lived in a gilded age. Having learned the secret of electricity from Edison and the "secret of combination" from J.P. Morgan at about the same time, the country powered along like a locomotive. The effect was compound, especially as they also knew the secret of the tariff. Soon they learned too the secret of the alternating current in motors (from a Serbian immigrant) and the secret of advertising and the secret of clubs, cabals and plutocracy. American business took everything before it, including the American labour movement.

Remarkable as it now seems, we who went to school in the conservative, anti-communist fifties and sixties were taught the history of Australian labour. We learnt about the rise of the trade unions and the Labor parties, as if it were inseparable from the rise of democracy. It was a legitimate, even heroic, part of Australian history. American labour never achieved the same status in American history. Had it been taught to Americans as it was taught to us, it would have been, as well as labour history, the history of staggering graft and corruption, spies, stooges and thugs, and the Winchester rifle and the baseball bat as instruments of political oppression; the history of Pinkertons Detective Agency whose employees in 1892, according to one historian, outnumbered the nation's standing army. It would have been, as they say, the downside — including the downside of mass immigration.

The more obvious presence of labour history in the story we were taught reflects not only our different experience but also different political values. In 1890s America, business, while brutally cracking the head of any worker in whom class consciousness was forming, gloated that it was "gradually subverting the power of the politician and rendering him subservient to its purposes". In Australia, Labor was incorporated into the system so thoroughly it formed one side of politics and the parliaments and one side of the political, social and industrial equation, and has done ever since. From the start both sides of politics agreed on the need for government intervention in the economy and society, including machinery to regulate the wages and conditions of labour. The consensus, described by Paul Kelly as the "Australian Settlement", was meliorist. Only recently has this broken down in the face of, first, financial deregulation and, more recently, labour market deregulation. Some might lament this and some might even hope to restore the government's role. It is unlikely that much can or will ever be done to reverse this process. The most useful thing is to recognise that in taking these decisions we took the biggest step we have ever taken towards the American social model. And this has profound implications for how we conceive of Australia and how we make it cohere.

5.   ... his vote is the desire of the politician – indeed, it is the very breath of the politician's being; the parliament exists to do the will of the workingman, and the Government exists to exercise it.

Mark Twain on Australia, 1897

> The difficulty to think at the end of the day
> When the shapeless shadow covers the sun
> And nothing is left except light on your fur ...

Wallace Stevens, A Rabbit as King of the Ghosts, quoted in Rabbit is Rich

The missing part in Rabbit's life is what he does with those little bits that feed the soul. Feed the mouth he can manage, though even that can go begging when Janice screws up with the meal. The lusts he can feed, in mind if not always in body. But what is there for the soul? And how does he get it? Not that we would want to change him into a liberal academic, a Brahmin or a union leader – he's cute the way he is. As Thelma says, he's "lovely".

For our purposes the vacancy for which Rabbit stands was the one left by the death of God and the inadequacy of all replacements. Rabbit is the problem anticipated by de Tocqueville: if you replace God with humanism and monarchs with the sovereignty of the people, to what will faith adhere? The answer was supposed to be, in part, a national ideal: democracy itself and all its heroes and history and rhetoric, its symbols, songs and flags. "I have never had a feeling politically that did not spring from the sentiments embodied in the Declaration of Independence," Lincoln once said. All these sentiments Americans have in abundance and work feverishly to maintain: the sacred texts of Jefferson and Lincoln worked over and over again, all the way down to that address delivered by George W. Bush to the joint sitting of Congress after the September 11 attack, which Ollie North, no less, within hours declared on CNN to be one of the greatest American speeches. The Americans long ago developed a natural dogma for the country and still breed up leaders who can regurgitate it at will.

But it was never enough by itself. That's where the little things make their entrance; the voluntary life of the nation that de Tocqueville believed was essential if democracy was not to turn into tyranny. He meant in particular those associations that fill the gap between the people and the executive power: the churches, the lodges, unions, interest groups and clubs (Rabbit and Janice have their golf club). With the exception of the golf club, all these have seriously withered, but gardens, sunrooms, sunken living rooms and ten times more than even Rabbit, much less de Tocqueville, could have imagined are there in models to suit every taste and pocket. All investments in ease and comfort for oneself and family are proof against despair and anarchy. How will a person fill his days? This is what the political question comes down to. How will the people or the nation advance? is academic by comparison. Our leaders now appear to understand this as a matter of political instinct. It is the stuff of politics as well as commerce. But the doctrine must accommodate a kind of paradox: whole-hearted pursuit of self-interest and ease and comfort is a step closer to American "individualism" and a step away from Australian "collectivism", "battlers" and the catch-phrase no Australian politician can resist, the "fair go". Not even resort to such fabulous mantras as "the greatest share-holding democracy in the world" will alter the trajectory. And so long as the little things that feed the soul, from Nike to the news, come straight out of the American blender, more and more of our days will be filled like Rabbit's.

Unfortunately, the equation is far from perfect. The blessings of a democracy, even one deemed sacred, do not satisfy everyone. People, especially Americans it seems, still pin their hopes on whatever can be made to seem *more* sacred: new, renovated and crank religions, nature and Thoreau, witch-hunts, conspiracy theories including those involving extra-terrestrial visitations (for which the FBI has a separate website), hallucinogens, the Body, the Mind, product brands.

> One Sabbath morn, as heavenward
> White Mountain tourists slowly spurred,
> On every rock, to their dismay,
> They read the legend all the way —
> SAPOLIO.

Sapolio was a brand of soap and Bret Harte wrote the verse about it in 1876. A century later, far from satirising them, Harry Angstrom is as addicted to comparing product brands as he is to comparing the different shapes and textures of different women's pubic thatch. It is by a process of comparison that he reaches the conclusion that America must be the happiest place on earth. And by the very same process we often hear Australians talk themselves into the same conclusion. In the course of an election campaign I was told by a man in a northern rivers town that, as Australia was the greatest country in the world, and this was the best town in Australia, and the bar of the Leagues Club where we stood at 11.00am in the morning while everyone was playing bingo was the best place in town, the square of maroon carpet on which we stood was the best square of carpet in the world. In fact these variations on Rabbit's reflection assume greater significance in Australia because, with little else to render "sacred" after the fair go and Gallipoli, the thought itself is one of the tablets of natural Aussie dogma.

Therein, surely lies the problem – or one of them. What is there to sacralise? Who is there to inhabit the pantheon? The very nature of our history, our traditional agnosticism, and the national character we so admire in ourselves mitigates against heroes. So our leaders are left saying that Donald Bradman is the greatest Australian – a leader of eleven men, who could use a bat like no other before or since, but could not bowl. An Australian Rabbit might put Bradman front and centre in his pantheon, but the American one would know that Babe Ruth and Jack Nicklaus don't belong with Lincoln. Harry knows there is something beyond sport and sex; he just can't concentrate for long enough to find it.

Who else goes in? The last man standing from the First World War? Phar Lap? John Curtin, and Menzies for balance? And what words are there to sing or recite or work over as the Americans do, so that every speech echoes Gettysburg? Henry Lawson has had his day and will not endure like Mark Twain – or Kipling for that matter. Henry Handel Richardson is admired principally by the "élites". Patrick White came too late, and is too difficult and writes more in reaction to Australia than on behalf of it. It is not because great deeds have not been done: it is that they do not amount to something articulate and powerful enough for the nation to gather around.

I can think of no better expression of this curious national inadequacy than the occasion of the first Keith Murdoch lecture in Melbourne this year. The speech, delivered by Keith Murdoch's son, Rupert, an American citizen, in the main concerned the Australian government's failure to spend enough on education and research. One could only applaud the sentiment; it is a scandalously poor record. But Murdoch's measure of this failure was entirely economic and comparative – as if he knew that his old countrymen only respond to their shortcomings when they are compared to the strengths of the Finns. Just as dispiritingly, not once did he mention the possibilities for personal growth and fulfilment, the advance of useful knowledge or the improvement of communities that for most of human history have been thought to inhere in education. Apparently not any more – education is a means of human capital formation.

Sharing the stage for the oration, spotlit in a glass case, was the armour worn by Ned Kelly; and when it was over guests were treated to a reading of Kelly's barmy "Jerilderie Letter", accompanied by Irish singing, dancing and mock punch-ups, and Nellie Melba warbling gorgeously. It was not that it was not done well, but it *was* a wonder it was done at all, there, at a fundraiser for the State Library of Victoria, to go with a speech about education, and much as it hurts to say this – that it was being done *again*.

The inadequacy of funding for education and research that Murdoch noted (he did not comment on the distribution of funding) is much more worrying than the lack of a sacred text or rites that the floor show somehow underlined. The lack of a decent research and education system *and* the presence of an expatriate modern media equivalent of John Pierpont Morgan to tell us about it is more worrying still – but it is possibly the fate of post-colonial societies to go on welcoming eminent foreigners and expatriates like royalty long after we have forgotten the reason for doing it.

All countries need a sacred story, or at least all peoples do. This country has a sacred story up to 1945 or so, even 1965. As with most other new-world countries it does not satisfy the indigenous people and won't until the story of their dispossession is persuasively included in it. Neither the present government, nor the present Opposition should it one day form a government, are likely to seriously attempt this: the government because it covets the votes of bigots and ignoramuses thinly disguised as "battlers" and is led by a man who refuses to believe the Aboriginal story or its legitimacy as Australian history; the Opposition because it just covets the votes. As a consequence many non-Aboriginal Australians will also find the story less than sacred or true, and with this disenchantment will go other articles of national faith. The pity of this is greater because, even without the Aboriginal component, the story is powerful and moving. It tells of a flourishing democracy, sentimentally, and in some important ways formally, attached to Great Britain (with a little help from the Americans recently), a continent tamed by hard work and ingenuity, not as it turned out to establish a new Britannia in another world but an Anglo-Saxon society of a distinctive Australian character; with sound institutions, a spirit of social progress, a facility to battle through, a loveable tendency to larrikinism, good sportsmen and even better soldiers. Gallipoli was the making of it, then the battlefields of France. There *was* an Australian pantheon emerging, and the war memorials built between the wars were a powerful and imaginative expression of it. Tobruk and Kokoda and Changi are bound to become part of the story if it can be kept alive.

A modest new memorial on the perimeter of the new Parliament House has a view of the mountains and plains under that huge Canberra sky. The inscription says, "Look around you, these are the things they believed in." This was the other part of the sacred text thus far – the love of the land and the prospect of owning a bit of it. It's the dream romanticised and sentimentalised by Henry Lawson in *Reedy River* and Banjo Paterson in *Clancy of the Overflow* – the open-air democracy. But the inscription tells a sadder tale. In fact, of all the memorials in Australia I think this new one is the most poignant. What catches in the throat is the past tense – it is the verbal equivalent of a distant crow or magpie. Those Australians did believe in something, and they died for it. That much of the text is sacred, and like the land itself it belongs as much to the good people of Carlton and Balmain as it does to John Howard or Les Murray or R.M. Williams and the good people of the bush who get around in his moleskins.

The problem is it's over. It does not connect in the way it once did. The American sacred story is also essentially over, but it connects through the Declaration, the flag, the republic and the ringing familiar words. To outsiders it's a little repellent and a long way from the truth, but it works, it stays alive. The Australian story does not work any more, or not well enough at least to hang the modern story on. A point has been reached where the words "fair go", "Gallipoli" and "show me a better country if you don't like this one" just don't do the job. The flag and the monarchy have reached a similar point. The existing panoply of symbols and mantras excludes too many people and too much of what has happened since the war – the migrants, Vietnam, the increase in the educated population, the beneficiaries and victims of the new economy, the new roles for women and new awareness of their roles in the past, a new awareness of the land. Australia now contains multitudes that the legend cannot accommodate. So long as our leaders ply the legend as if it *can* accommodate them, the further we drift from the truth about ourselves. It is quite possible to win political contests without confronting this truth, or by encouraging all sorts of false sentiment or turning ignorance and resentment to advantage. But the country loses. At times in our post-war history, our political imagination has matched the social and economic forces working on the nation and its consciousness. There have been times when the future became the main interest. But each time the bird was caught, stilled. Just now it might as well be dead.

If the country has a problem, so has John Howard. He has been trying to stuff a pluralist, post-modern bird into a pre-modern cage. The bird won't go. It's not that it won't fit, but rather that it's not a bird. It's no one thing. It's our multitudes. During his years in Opposition he called forth a class of people he called "battlers" – ciphers or ghosts of the pre-1945 Australia with echoes of the Depression, the forgotten people of R.G. Menzies, the diggers of the First World War and the goldfields, cobbers. And as the battlers were glorified, another nebulous class was vilified. These were the "élites". It gave the battlers better definition to encourage images of effete, opinionated bleeding hearts chattering on the pavements while real people did the work and battled. Labor leapt on the idea like a sloth falling from a tree and soon they too were praising the "battlers" who loathed them, and loathing the chatterers who would lay down their lives for them. Strange to dismiss from your ranks the educated, the open-minded, the moderately thoughtful and reflective – and brand them for good measure. The archetypes of this political strategy are authoritarian, which is to say brutal and stupid. With both parties employing it here, the value of the tactic in a liberal democracy is hard to judge. Can we call it a success if one party wins with it and the other loses? On the other hand, it seems fairly certain that few benefits will flow to the country itself in the long term – and few to the political parties, dare we say. On the contrary, the effect has been to give ignorance at least the same value as education, likewise bigotry and tolerance, creativity and crassness, past realities and the present one. Much that a country – and a society – needs, including the capacity to imagine, to regenerate and reinvent itself, has been discounted. It's a strategy to honour every Rabbit in Australia.

In conjunction with eccentric policy priorities like half-strangling the ABC and suffocating the universities, it is also a policy to imitate the original Rabbit. That is to say, to imitate the hole in America. Harry Angstrom lives the American dream and finds it hollow at the centre, much as President Bush's war on terrorism speech was hollow at the centre – platitudes, phrases whose meaning had been leached out of them, tacked together like a henhouse, to borrow from George Orwell. Rabbit finds, and his life gives expression to the discovery, that the same thing has happened to religion – they have taken God out of it; as they took the individual out of individualism and put conformity in its place; as they took labour out of capitalism, liberalism out of enlightenment, the world out of worldliness and the taste out of food. Rabbit doesn't get it. The Americans don't get it. Watch CNN for half an hour – or even more alarming, Fox News – and try not to say, "They don't get it." And what is almost beyond understanding, this from a country of matchless resources and institutions and ideals and genius.

6.   Far better it is to dare mighty things, to win glorious triumphs, even though checkered by failure, than to rank with those poor spirits who neither enjoy much or suffer much, because they live in that gray twilight that knows not victory nor defeat.

Theodore Roosevelt, 1899

Only occasionally is an American leader as frank as Grover Cleveland was back in 1896. "[We] have a concern with [Cuba] which is by no means of a wholly sentimental or philanthropic character," he said. His words captured something about America that should help us see more truly the nature of our position and, more importantly, encourage us to think about what it might be in a decade or two. The same might be said of Teddy Roosevelt, the most gung ho of all American presidents. He is quoted by way of advocating that, saddled as we are with the Americans one way or another, we make the best of it and don't go like Rabbit shambling towards the void. This country does have choices. One of them is to follow the US as if her motives really are wholly sentimental or philanthropic; the other is to be as clear-eyed and self-interested as they are about things. Even if both positions produced the same material result, there is still more to be said for pursuing the second one because more dignity and less of the gray twilight attaches to it.

The second course, being based on a realistic assessment of the American position, might lead us to a more realistic – and fruitful – assessment of our own. Let us say, for instance, that we make it a rule of life with our ally that we attempt to emulate only the greatness in American society, we still cannot recreate the history from which the greatness sprang, and we would not want to. (We can have their music but not their slaves.) We know that our material and human resources cannot compare to theirs. In fact we are so unlike each other, it is almost impossible to think of ànything they do that we could do as well while remaining consistent with our character. Their tradition of great benefactions to public institutions, for instance, conflicts with our tradition of reliance on government funding – and while it is possible to increase the proportion of private to public in this country, there is also a danger that any success will be seized on by governments keen to rid themselves of yet more obligations to society. It is true the very rich in Australia don't put as much back as they do in America, but perhaps they don't take as much out. On a more abstract plane, we could aim to be as full of confidence and hope as they are, but only at the risk of losing that weary fatalism by means of which we understand each other and charm the world. We could wave the flag like they do, but it's a loathsome habit and, in any case, the flag is not all ours. Imitation is too close to flattery and flattery makes us look like flunkies.

Better to avoid what we don't like in the Americans, and here Rabbit provides a useful negative example. Take his patriotism: it is mainly vapid because patriotism nearly always is, and American patriotism is particularly vapid. All patriotism looks backward, and with a distorting mirror. Lacking both their history and their myths as well as any satisfactory "sacred text", we could do the sensible thing – we could make the guiding principles of Australia its diversity and pluralism, its inorganicness, the absence of oppressive and constraining symbols (the flag and the monarchy, for example, are meaningless), and seize the chance to create a post-modern republic or a "republic of opportunity" as Guy Rundle called it in the last Quarterly Essay – and a very civilised society. Australia is as much a lifestyle as it is a nation – we should make the nation in that image. As for the sacred text, the natural dogma, the ruling ideology – let it be the old one, but let it also be whatever exists now and whatever we have in mind for the future. Oscar Wilde, who loathed the "materialising spirit" he saw in America, wrote in *The Soul of Man under Socialism*: "It is with the future that we have to deal. For the past is what man should not have been. The present is what man ought not to be. The future is what artists are." It is a more useful philosophy now than it was when he thought of it. For artist, read imagination and creativity, and then read just about any American whiz on the future. The whizzes are in tune with Wilde: those two commodities of artists (if not artists themselves), plus skills and knowledge, will be like diamonds. An Australia whose guiding principle was possibility, and that valued intelligence and skill more than it has in recent years, might actually revive the sentiment last uttered a century ago – that, with America, it was the hope of humankind.

The same kind of Australia would also return to the position of just a few years back when it maintained a healthy friendship with the United States while engaging vigorously with the countries of Asia. Our security does not appear to be more assured in proportion to our retreat from that policy, but our horizons do seem to be lower, and with them our sense of possibility less tangible. Again it feels like the Rabbit syndrome: camped by the burrow or halfway down it. And as night follows day, timidity becomes fear and fear becomes hostility, and with so much feeling pumping in our own veins, suddenly we can't or don't imagine what's happening in others, even though their distress is obvious and much greater than ours. Acts unconscionable to generous, confident and brave people – that is to say, people more like Australians four or five years ago – become justifiable and necessary.

Emptiness is the great danger. If the little things that feed the soul are the same here as they were in Rabbit's Brewster, Penn. c.1985 then we are headed for mediocrity and have no hope of delivering on our promise. Perhaps we can feed our souls with stock market shares and new technology and Gatorade, but there are signs that both sides of politics now sense that something more is needed. This sense may have arisen from the experience of tramping round the fading provinces and towns, hearing people repeatedly state their need to be useful as individuals and as communities. It was one of the lessons of politics: how a prevailing ideology shuts out the oldest, most rudimentary observations about society and human nature, and even when they are clearly pointed out will not permit them to enter. After years in denial it transpires that there is such a thing as a need for recognition after all; and also a need to be useful to one's fellows or at least to oneself. Individual and community effort is undoubtedly the key to meeting these needs, but governments that want to build a bridge back to the people will find a useful part to play. For those who do, the possibilities are almost infinite. But we should not expect too much too soon; it takes a long time to turn around a train of thought. Until that happens we can expect the federal government to pursue whatever policies they reckon match the idea of turning Australia into "the greatest shareholding democracy in the world". It is a sterling ambition, but constitutes such a narrow and perverse definition of democracy as to be either impossible to achieve or pointless. It is also very like making the Declaration of Independence the foundation of your belief and then shrinking from the word "liberal".

7.   Let us have faith that right makes might, and in that faith, let us, to
the end, dare to do our duty as we understand it.

Abraham Lincoln, 27 February 1860

Refugees frighten us. Reconciliation with Aborigines, native title, a republic – these things consistently prove too much for us. If Australia cannot face the truth that its life is its own and no one else's, then we should deal with the fear. It will not do to weld the negative and reactionary sentiments in the community into some kind of ideological truncheon to wave at intruders and frighten off internal opposition. We can't piece this mood together with the modern pluralist society *and* try to make it all cohere around the bathos of very old men and a semi-mythic military catastrophe in Turkey. If it has in fact been calculated that this refurbished fantasy is good politics or the best we can do with the place, if this is to be our disposition and identity, the best we can imagine, it must be a symptom of a greater need. And if that need is security, and we no longer want to find it on our own, there is but one remedy. Far better than playing America's deputy in Southeast Asia, a region from whose forums we are comprehensively excluded, let us petition for inclusion in the American union. Demand it.

We are not disposed to live alone, obviously, so let us live with them. Would we have less respect in the world? No, we would have more, and we would have much more respect in Washington – we would have Congressmen, possibly even Cabinet members. Think of what we would gain. More dignity, more influence and more peace of mind. It's all upside, surely. No more fifty-cent dollars. No more current account nightmare. We can amortise the debt. Let us integrate fully with the world's biggest economy and take our place under the missile shield. If they'll go to war over New York, they'll go to war over every State. It's much better than ANZUS. No agonising foreign policy decisions, no more excruciating arguments about the national identity. The cultural cringe ends the day we join. We're talking freedom here – a bloodless revolution and one straight out of the end-of-history handbook.

We should put it to them straight, like a business deal. It's not as if there's no upside for them. They get a State instead of a colony. They can go on pretending they're not imperialists, but we won't have to go on pretending our soul's our own. It's win–win if ever there was such a thing. Frankly it's hard to see a better idea coming up this side of 2010 – and if we wait any longer than that there'll be no deal to strike. We'll be begging them to have us.

That's the first option. It means jettisoning both the republic and the monarchy – which happens to be another argument for doing it. Should Costello or Crean become prime minister, there will be something weird and contradictory about backing out of Asia and into the deputy's role and urging a republic at the same time. But this is not the only reason why a republic is less attractive than it used to be. The "irritable patriotism" exemplified by Hanson and swallowed up by Howard, the new xenophobia and meanness, the retreat to Fortress Australia, all bode badly for a republic. The chances are it would reflect this mood. The new Australia might be too much like the old one created with a White Australia policy and other more easily understood phobias a century ago. The symmetry is too striking, the risk is too great: particularly as the people continue to resolutely oppose appointing the Head of State by any method other than popular election. This would so change the character of Australian democracy, and so politicise the Head of State that large numbers of republicans could not vote for it. Seeing the truth of this might save the country from this ultimate Americanisation, but imagine if it didn't. Far from the light and liberating post-modern republic on offer in the nineties, with power more diffuse and openness a byword, we will find ourselves with power more concentrated and the present xenophobia and tinny nationalism enshrined in it. The republic, remember, was to put the icing on the cake: it was to confirm the best in us, not the worst.

There remains the option of the status quo, insofar as it can be called that while Britain hurries to look more like an American vassal than we do. In view of the souring of Australia the monarchy is not such a bad option any more. It is a timid course, but Australians just now *are* timid, as well as cantankerous, and the timid are always more likely to vote away their liberties. Something as silly as the present arrangement is appropriate in the present circumstances, even if we wake up one morning and find Charles and Camilla on our throne. It's a pity they come from where they do, that's all. If only they were American it would be perfect. Bill Clinton comes to mind.

SOURCES

Essay sources and occasional supplementary material are given below. Page numbers indicate where the quotes, etc. appear.

3   Thurber quoted in William Appleman Williams, *The Roots of the Modern American Empire*, Random House, New York, 1969, p. 439.

7   Menzies on blood in R.G. Menzies, *The International Situation in 1935*, Australian Institute of International Affairs, Melbourne, 1935.

9   Cleveland quoted in W.A. Williams, *op. cit.* pp. 377–78.

11   Mrs Smith to Angstrom, p. 81. All page references to the first three books in the Rabbit quartet are from *A Rabbit Omnibus*, Penguin, Harmondsworth, Middlesex, 1991.

12   On Robin Boyd, see Geoffrey Serle, *Robin Boyd: A Life*, Melbourne University Press, Melbourne, 1995, p. 329.

15   Others see in Updike's Rabbit novels a projection of Updike's own political conservatism. In recent years both Gary Wills and Gore Vidal have savaged him mercilessly as the arch American reactionary.

17   Jill's words from *Rabbit Redux* in *A Rabbit Omnibus*, p. 312.

17   Ruth's words from *Rabbit Run*, p. 174 and *Rabbit is Rich*, p. 526 (in *A Rabbit Omnibus*).

18   On the pursuit of happiness and small things, see de Tocqueville, *On Democracy in America*, qv. in Adam Gopnik, "The Habit of Democracy", *New Yorker*, 11 November 2001.

18 On the Rabbit quartet as a critique, see Joyce Carol Oates, review of *Rabbit at Rest*, *New York Times Book Review*, 30 September 1990.

19-20 See Lewis Lapham, "Dies Irae", in *Waiting for the Barbarians*, Verso, New York, 1997.

30 Film treatments of Billy the Kid include *The Left Handed Gun* (1958); *Pat Garrett and Billy the Kid* (1973); *One Eyed Jacks* (1961] *Gore Vidal's Billy the Kid* (1989, from a 1955 TV play).

30-31 Cormac McCarthy from *Blood Meridian*, Picador, London, 1990, p. 53.

31 On practical paganism and moral enlightenment see Michael Roe in Frank Crowley (ed.), *A New History of Australia*, Heinemann, Melbourne, 1974, pp. 110–112.

31 On religious sects and present-day American politics, see Andrew Delbanco, *The Real American Dream, A Meditation on Hope*, Harvard University Press, Cambridge, Mass., 1999.

32 On George W. Bush and Darwinism and Creationism in schools, see Frederick Crews, "Saving Us from Darwin", *New York Review of Books*, 4 October 2001.

36-37 See Menzies Papers NLA MS4936, series 6 box 251.

37 "My strength is yours" from R.G. Menzies, *Australia's Place in the Empire*, 1932, reprinted from *International Affairs*, July–August 1935.

38 On the *Shenendoah*, see K.S. Inglis, *The Australian Colonists: An Exploration of Social History 1788–1870*, Melbourne University Press, Melbourne, 1974, pp. 228–30.

39   On Pinkertons, see Jeremy Brecher, *Strike!*, Straight Arrow Books, San Francisco, 1972, p. 55.

40   On "subverting the power of the politician", see *Bankers Magazine* 1901, quoted in William Miller, *A New History of the United States*, London, 1970, p. 259.

50   Cleveland quoted in W.A. Williams, *op. cit.* p. 406.

THE OPPORTUNIST | *Correspondence*

Relentlessly Unhip to the Very End
John Birmingham

A version of this article was first published in the *Age*, 3 November 2001.

They looked like Bjork fans. You know, way cooler than you or me. They were tucked away in the corner of an impossibly hip indie cafe at the north end of Bondi, one of the spiritual homes of the chattering classes, or the new élite. Call them what you will. They sat there early in the election knocking back the muffins and lattés and broadcasting their views about the *Tampa* crisis to all within earshot. I sat nearby and listened with amazement as these three latté Nazis agreed that if the refugee ships coming from Indonesia would not turn around, some would definitely have to be sunk. And perhaps a couple of Afghans might need to be shot too. One of them, henna tattoos, nose rings and all, volunteered that she was up to the job.

It was a political moment of fantastic incongruity – even more so than John Howard's housing policy photo-op with that earnest, bizarrely haired neo-punk couple. It neatly demonstrates one of the weird inversions which have made this campaign so difficult for Kim Beazley. If, as reported, Peter Reith really did say that war would be the only issue in the election, then this sort of scene – played out endlessly in cafés, pubs, on buses and, of course, across the airwaves via talkback – will have loomed large in Howard's reckoning.

It certainly dominated the imagery of his campaign launch in Sydney last weekend. As the faithful took their places in the recital hall, a giant slide show featured happy snaps of the Prime Minister with George Bush, East Timor peacekeepers and military personnel bound for the Afghanistan conflict. The set was spare, the tone was sombre. The message, not entirely subliminal, was safety and security. Howard was more upbeat than he had been in the first two weeks of the campaign, but a restrained air prevailed.

Television is not kind to Howard. The broadcast of his speech did not do his performance justice. There is something in the compressing effect of TV which diminishes his presence, makes him seem smaller than he really is. His voice, nasal and flat, can sound more defensive and even petulant than it should. His limitations haunted him throughout the 1980s but he has made them into something of a weapon in the later years of his public life. He is more natural in person, less the caricature we are used to, and he is more at ease with ordinary people than they often are with him. Two young teenage boys – "of Middle Eastern appearance" as the saying goes – who chanced across a press conference in his suburban campaign office last weekend were left star struck and grinning like the dumber models at a motor show when he bounded over to schmooze them for the cameras.

To visit his campaign office is to enter a small monument to the determinedly ordinary. It is a temporary space, rented on the ground floor of a failed homecraft business, but the dowdiness seems almost purposeful. The decor consists of a few blue and white partially deflated balloons, old worn carpet, faded Whitlam-era wallpaper of astounding ugliness, pine panelling and cheap cast-off plastic furniture. The whole scene is of a kind with Howard's relentlessly unhip image.

Understand one thing, though. He is not an ordinary man, no matter how much he might cloak himself in the cardigan of middle-class respectability. He is a thousand miles removed from being boring or grey or even conservative. He is a fascinating study, as worthy of consideration as his arch-nemesis Keating. He inspires passions every bit as powerful and profane. In him, as in Keating, we find the best and worst of ourselves.

That's right. The best.

Let's start there, since it is the road less travelled.

Our politics are brutal. Not bloodthirsty, or primitive, but totally lacking in pity for any hint of weakness or human frailty. Howard knows this down in his meat, where the damage lies. Old wounds he has aplenty; the deepest of them, the thickest, most hardened scars, he took from allies, not enemies. He understands betrayal in the most bitter and intimate of ways. In a way that we who have lived normal lives can only guess at and shudder.

Consider the witless beserkers of the Joh-for-PM campaign, who stormed out of Queensland and destroyed any chance he had of taking the prime ministership from Bob Hawke. Remember Andrew Peacock's cabal of assassins, who stole upon him with knives in hand, like Brutus and the Senators upon Julius; traitors who, not satisfied with merely plunging in the blade, then had to gloat over their treachery in the most obscene and public fashion. Can you even begin to imagine the extremes of humiliation and helpless rage to which they subjected him? Can you make the leap of empathy from the worst betrayal you have ever known, at the hand of a friend or family member or lover, and magnify it a hundred times over, with the whole world watching?

It would likely destroy you.

And yet there he was, never retiring from the field, simply binding up the wounds and standing to, ready for battle again. With one cautious eye to the rear, for sure, never really trusting those around him. Making a list and checking it twice. But there, like the ancient mariner clinging to life as the tempest ebbs around him, or harking to Shelley's howl in *Prometheus Unbound*, neither to change nor falter nor repent, but just bear up and hope "till Hope creates from its own wreck the thing it contemplates". His survival and triumph given the relentless hostility directed against him speaks of a weird, almost Nietzschean willpower. That which does not kill me can only make me fit for public office.

Beneath this refusal to surrender in the face of overwhelming odds you can find, if you care to look, faint echoes of our creation myths; the stoic perseverance on the frontier, at Gallipoli or Kokoda. This is not to make some fatuous and embarrassing link between the courage needed to charge up the Nek and that required to show your face on television after being comprehensively outclassed by a hapless soufflé like Andrew Peacock. Rather it is to admit that Howard is sincere in his worship of the old Australian virtues because they inspire him and give him strength far beyond anything conceded by his opponents or those many, many Australians numbered amongst the ranks of the new élites – a group for whom there is but one perfect word to describe their feelings about the Prime Minister. Appalled.

It is a confounding irony of his administration that Howard should have been the one to deliver on two shibboleths of the old Left and the new élite. Gun control and East Timor. In forcing through the former despite the savage and sometimes unhinged opposition from sections of his own natural constituency, he demonstrated that unshakeable commitment to a principle which, in other circumstances, would so infuriate opponents in the Labor Party, on the waterfront, in the women's, green or gay movements. In shepherding the country through the latter crisis, a potential catastrophe of historic proportions, he achieved what no Labor leader had ever come close to: the deployment in East Timor of an Australian military shield behind which the benighted people of that island could come to freedom at last. Of course it is in the interest of the ALP to downplay Howard's role, and to emphasise the many tactical and strategic blunders his government made in the months leading up to the ballot which undeniably made the final conflagration worse. But in the end it was John Howard, not Gough Whitlam, Bob Hawke or Paul Keating who took up the sword and shield.

As he flies around the country, rattling sabres and showering largesse on the new-born and the geriatric, it is tempting, post-*Tampa*, to view his campaign in the most cynical fashion. Guy Rundle, in the recently released *Quarterly Essay, The Opportunist*, puts forward the most coherent and aggressive analysis of this sort. In Rundle's view, having long ago lost any chance with the small, but significant minority forming the new élites, Howard decided it was better to "go in hard and summon up the worst side of the Australian spirit". It is a view of the PM shared at the other end of the ideological spectrum by journals such as the *Wall Street Journal* and the *Economist*, illustrating that strange alliance of interests now arrayed against him.

But Rundle errs in perceiving in Howard our own Richard Nixon, a man distanced as a politician from his own beliefs and morality. The key to Howard is not his cynicism but his sincerity. Certainly he is astute and knows only too well the power of the symbols and emotions he has been manipulating since the *Tampa* hove into view. The triumphalist roar which greeted his introduction of Philip Ruddock to the Liberals' formal campaign launch in Sydney spoke eloquently, if brutishly, of the mortal harm which the refugee crisis had done to the ALP. That room full of well-fed white people knew they had been resurrected by Howard and his principle spear-carrier. Just as Lazarus himself had recovered from his triple bypass to seize the reins of the party, and then the government, after the bitter and barren years of the early 1990s.

However, to think of Howard as some cold, amoral tactician playing with the lives of refugees for personal gain is to fundamentally misunderstand his nature. He is a believer. To some it seems grotesque to describe his stand on asylum seekers as principled, because of the terrible human cost, the bizarre political contortions, the monstering of the Pacific micro-states and, of course, because of the massive boost it gives to Howard's own chance of retaining government – the obvious self-interest involved. But when he talks about the principle of controlling the nation's borders it is not just political expediency. He believes in what he is doing even as he consciously and happily reaps the electoral benefit. In this he is a sincere and utter bastard.

This duality of Howard's is in part what so bewilders his cultural enemies. We cannot see his championing of the monarchy as nationalism, for instance, only betrayal. We can see nothing of his own background – his own father's battle to secure a modest but solid future for his family – in

Howard's preference for practical Aboriginal reconciliation emphasising health, education and the provision of basic services over symbolic atonement. We see only the punisher and straightener.

And of course we see a racist.

Of all the charges levelled against him, this is the one that wounds most deeply, which brings forth that peevish lower lip and belligerent defensiveness. It will haunt him forever. His Labor opponents will be ever ready to insinuate the worst. Those Australians who loathe him as much as Keating was ever loathed will always believe it, particularly as his continued success flies in the face of everything they hold dear.

What is truly in his heart? Only he can know. But it may well be that he is not the demon of modern political mythology. His genius, as David Marr wrote, might simply lie in seeing us not as we would like to be, but exactly as we are.

John Birmingham

THE OPPORTUNIST | *Correspondence*

Paul Bongiorno

I am sure that John Howard would not baulk at Guy Rundle's description of him as "The Opportunist". Opportunism and pragmatism are features of John Howard's public life as is an intense self-belief in his destiny to be prime minister. I remember travelling with him to Israel in 1989 when he was opposition leader. While there, the news came from Australia that Fred Chaney had expressed interest in leading the Liberals, "if John Howard fell under a bus". This merely gave voice to rumblings within the party that Howard wasn't really taking them anywhere. In conversation, Mr Howard refused to countenance the idea that anyone then in the party, Peacock or Chaney included, was better able to lead the party than he. It's a tribute to his tenacity and persistence that he hung on through the Peacock coup, and then the Hewson and Downer leaderships, to be finally given his next big chance.

Howard's self-belief goes to his sense that the values he espouses, traditional Anglo-Protestant virtues that built an empire and founded this nation, are absolutes that still underpin Australia's identity and success. Rundle nicely captures this in his essay but I believe that in exploring Howard's opportunism we need to also look at its moral underpinnings.

And here we get a clue from his deathbed visit to B.A. Santamaria. The fundamentalist, Catholic, anti-Communist was much admired by the Prime Minister, and the two share a doctrine that neither would necessarily admit to but to which their actions bear ample testimony, namely, that the ends justify the means. Santamaria once remarked that you do not use Marquis of Queensberry rules in the fight against atheistic Communists. Howard would say the same of fighting opponents whose motto is "whatever it takes". So whatever it takes to stay in power is exonerated by the exercise of that power to protect a world order that is True and Good or at least closer to what is True and Good than any alternatives.

At the height of the *Tampa* crisis, the Reverend Tim Costello wrote a highly critical piece in the *Sydney Morning Herald* concerning the immorality of using human beings as a means to an end. He tore apart, philosophically and theologically, the Howard argument that we have to treat the asylum seekers in this way as a deterrent to others. The reverend gentleman went on to argue from Matthew's gospel the Christian belief that, "Whatsoever you do to the least of my brothers you do to me," and further that, "I was naked and you clothed me, hungry and you fed me, homeless and you took me in." I raise this because I detected in the Rundle essay an implied innocence-by-association linking Howard's heir apparent with his professionally Christian brother. The Rundle conclusion seemed to be that things can only get better under Peter Costello. We can all live in this hope but the Treasurer, like the Prime Minister, is more likely to believe that politics is the art of the possible and that, as Gough Whitlam once remarked, only the impotent are pure.

There is no doubt that Howard is one of the finest practitioners of the art of politics we've seen. It is refreshing to see someone of Rundle's perspicacity acknowledging this while at the same time lamenting that these skills are employed with a ruthlessness that in the end helps to destroy the very values they paradoxically believe they serve.

Paul Bongiorno

THE OPPORTUNIST | Correspondence

Christopher Pearson

One of the first casualties of the Culture Wars in the 1960s was civility. Previously it had been quite commonplace for husbands and wives to disagree passionately about politics and religion without abiding rancour and for lifelong friends to be in lifelong disputation.

May I say at the outset that I bear Guy Rundle no resentment over the many issues where we differ deeply. He is a worthy sparring partner, and one of the regular columnists in the *Adelaide Review* (which I edit) whom we're proud to publish. His particular distinction, in *Arena Magazine* and elsewhere, is to re-invent and rehabilitate the Left as a political project. Characteristically his approach is subtle, genuinely funny — a rarer commodity on the Left than many would like to imagine — and prepared to confront inconvenient facts.

It grieves me that his admittedly polemical *Quarterly Essay* on John Howard (*The Opportunist*) falls short on civility, subtlety and engagement with the facts. I found it more bilious than enlightening. Peter Craven, in his Introduction, claims that one of Rundle's distinctive starting points is that, unlike so many of his colleagues and contemporaries he's "not offended by the Prime Minister's personal style". Yet he summons up the tension between Howard's sensibility brought "eyeball-to-eyeball with a sensibility, at once mordant and self-involved, that cannot *believe* all this drivel about Family, Mateship and the bloody picket fence". He calls it "an attempt to understand the kind of mind that could see political advantage in such pity and such terror" as *Tampa* and September 11 evoked.

Rundle himself calls Howard "the short-trousered boy-man striding through a series of foreign capitals like Tintin". The allusion is presumably to the classic demeaning stereotype of the schoolmaster – "a man among boys, a boy among men". He reinforces the notion of immaturity and directionlessness some paragraphs later: "the *Tampa* crisis will hang around his neck as he wanders the world" – an amalgam of the Ancient Mariner and the Flying Dutchman.

The adjectives "shoddy" and "cynical" are often deployed. Rundle's case is that Howard relied on grotesque, unscrupulous tactics to win the election and "some very dark corners of the Australian psyche".

Ad hominem abuse is a poor substitute for fact-based argument, no matter how therapeutic it may be for the author and many of his readers. Let's consider a few of those Derridean obdurate facts which Guy Rundle leaves out of his analysis.

First there is the fact that some 1,684 people suspected of serious criminal offences unrelated to their means of entry were detained in refugee camps last year. There's little doubt that some of them were engaging in the routine practice of spying on exiles from their own countries. Nor is there any reason to doubt that there is also routine exploitation of migrant enclaves, detained or at large, whether by evangelism, the enlistment of passive support or coercion via threats to relatives still overseas. Among the detainees was a known mass murderer who was a high-ranking officer in the Iraqi secret police. This is a matter of public record.

Second, there is the well-documented movement of various and sundry terrorist organisations out of the Middle East, where the spectre of the war of all against all is an increasing problem, into softer target locations in Southeast Asia, notably Indonesia, Malaysia and the Philippines. The Deputy Chief of the Indonesian Army, General Kiki Syahnakri, has repeatedly warned of their presence in the region. Indonesia's border control in an unstable archipelago is at best vestigial and Syahnakri has been outspoken about the presence of bin Laden associates in Indonesia and their recruitment of local militants. Is it likely that Islamic fundamentalists in the mutinous areas of the Philippines and in Malaysia aren't also, as the local Asian press has so often reported, being invited to join the Jihad?

One of the commonplaces of national security debate is that for at least the last decade there has been a transformation in the way that international terrorism functions. As Rohan Gunaratna, a Senior Fellow at St Andrews University Centre for the Study of Terrorism (Scotland) puts it: "there's been a change not only in the location but the tactics and focus of political violence." It's now aimed "especially at Western targets in most vulnerable areas, such as Asia ... and by intermingling with refugee and migrant flows, terrorist groups have established their presence ... especially in liberal democracies like Australia ... They operate through front cover and sympathetic organisations, taking the face of human rights and humanitarian groups." As he also notes, one of the crueller ironies is that their interventions in aid of the poor are often very effective.

Rundle no doubt distrusts anything coming out of the Murdoch press instinctively, but it's worth mentioning that the *Australian* reported (30 October) that "bin Laden's men are here." It confirmed that ASIO had uncovered substantial evidence about terrorist cells just before the

Olympic Games and that a number of bin Laden's known associates were being investigated. It also repeated the disturbing report that telephone records showed that the Muslim extremists who bombed the World Trade Center back in 1993 had made multiple calls to Australian numbers, believed to be in a cluster of terrorist safe houses in New South Wales.

Apart from the bin Laden connection, Gunaratna cites a number of other terrorist groups known to have an Australian presence. They include the pro-Palestinian Hamas, the Lebanese Hezbollah, two separate Punjabi outfits (the International Sikh Youth Federation and the Barbacosa), the Tamil Tigers, the Chechnyan Mujaheddin and the IRA.

According to Gunaratna – and it's a view broadly accepted within the Office of the National Assessments and Military Intelligence circles – Asian-based terrorism has a new-found tendency to mutate rapidly, when it moves into host countries, from support structures to operational infra-structures.

In Canada, for example, the Barbacosa bombed an Air India plane leaving for India in 1985, killing 329 passengers, including many Canadians. More recently, Ahmed Ressam claimed refugee status in Canada via a lax "touch soil" policy much like our own. In 1999 he was arrested crossing the US border with a truckload of plastic explosives. These details and the analysis based on them have been public knowledge for months and in some cases for years. I've drawn heavily in this reply to Rundle on a column of mine published in the *Financial Review* earlier this year.

On the question of the *Tampa* incident, the US Deputy Secretary of State specifically referred to it at the time as a security concern because people who could gain asylum having destroyed their passports would obviously use those strategies, as well as flying in people in business suits with expertly forged papers, if infiltration by stealth rather than immediate political violence was being planned.

What Guy Rundle's highly emotive account of the *Tampa* boat people omits to mention is that almost all the adult males (quite understandably) had crude, lethal weapons. When the *Tampa* captain spoke of the ease with which a group more than ten times the number of his crew could overpower them he was entirely serious. According to the law of the sea, when rescue victims issue threats, enforce demands and essentially take over the running of a ship, it's hijacking or, more precisely, piracy. That they were desperate and determined enough to take the law into their own hands is a plea in mitigation, not a defence.

Even if one were prepared to accept that Howard and Beazley's initial response to the *Tampa* incident was heartless and cynical – a proposition which I don't for a moment accept – the accusation would be beside the point. What Rundle fails to consider is the question of whether Australia has discernible national interests, which override humanitarian concerns regarding an (in all probability) otherwise blameless majority of this boatload of illegal immigrants.

The Left habitually dodges the notion of the national interest, as Rundle has in this case, even though it is far more compelling an argument than "our international obligations" as defined by UN treaties of the most Mickey Mouse kind. It's of a piece with the internationalist habit of mind that refuses to engage in complex arguments about moral law and obligations outside a Genevan reference point.

It seems to me that the Left want to avoid a prudential debate on the merits of particular cases and the evidence of real and present danger to the State in favour of one founded on moral absolutes, couched in humanitarian Newspeak but largely unexamined. The deployment of terms like "social justice", an oxymoronic notion if ever there was one, is symptomatic.

Meanwhile, on other major moral questions, Rundle and his allies hysterically assert a consequentialist ethic on "safe injecting rooms", drugs policy generally, abortion, bioethics and family law. Selective moralism is the last refuge of polemicists, apart perhaps from sneering. They want to claim that Howard's policy, and Beazley's incoherent bet-each-way echo of it are wrong ethically rather than merely mistaken or impractical. No doubt it's rhetorically easier and more satisfying; cheap shots that will go down well with their subdivision of the true believers.

Nonetheless there are questions about international terrorism and Australia as a soft target which won't disappear simply by wishing them away or disregarding them, and they are urgent questions. The transparent snobbery of deriding Howard for being shorter than Keating, or because his wife doesn't have a paid job, or Pauline Hanson for that matter because of her mangled pronunciation of "Australia" isn't even the beginning of an answer.

Craven, in his Introduction, says: "Rundle's is a dazzling fragmented portrait, more like a de Kooning than a Lucian Freud, because the portraitist keeps having to retrieve himself from his own obsessive technical problems that threaten to swamp his sense of the subject ..."

This strikes me as inordinately kind. Rundle's argument is kaleidoscopic in its representation of its subject. To put it another way, the essay is a catalogue aria of all the failings, real and imagined, of Australian Liberalism, conservatism generally and John Howard. It's kaleidoscopic in the sense that the elements of the argument resolve themselves into patterns as reassuringly symmetrical as the world does when viewed through a Marxian theoretical prism. Notions like "progress" and "reaction" are used as though, assured of certain certainties, they could be relied on as conveying meaning – with no need for qualification – where they strike me as buzzwords of long ago.

Historical determinism is used in much the same way. This is disappointing because at his best Rundle is as concerned and effective as anyone on his side of the argument about purifying the dialect of the tribal discourse about politics. Again, when he claims that political correctness is "a usefully 'spectral' political force – its opponents brought it into being simply by mentioning it", he does less than justice to his own powers of observation. He claims that: "By no fair assessment could it be said [of native title arguments and the Zeitgeist in the early '90s] to be a debate in which there was an attempt to stifle discussion."

No one listening to ABC Radio National or attending a tertiary institution during that era could have failed to see evidence of stifled debate. The lack of pluralism in the case of the ABC is still breathtakingly conspicuous. Either Rundle has fallen into the terrible trap of the polemicist – becoming incapable of distinguishing between one's own propaganda and things as they are – or he's trespassing on our good nature.

There is one important point on which I partially agree with him about Howard – the incompatibility of libertarian economic policies and "the idea of a bounded and stable social order". Rundle says, "Howard refuses to recognise that the former is now the principal enemy of the latter," (an issue of which he is increasingly well aware) and identifies him as "first and foremost a servant of a corporate world".

The contradictions between the conservative/liberal and economic libertarian world views are real enough. One of the interesting things about Howard is that he has become increasingly less doctrinaire about dry economics, less the slave of some long-dead economist, and more flexible and pragmatic than the dry commentators can find it in themselves to forgive.

By this I don't simply mean the time-honoured expedient of "buying off the sugar seats in Queensland", as one National Party minister rather bluntly puts it. I mean that he is less driven by any abstract notions of how Australia should do business than a concern that the part of the economy governments can manage or influence are managed as well as they can be, given the vagaries of domestic politics and our place in the world economy.

The idea that Howard is primarily a servant of the corporate world is a familiar nostrum of the Left. I think that in fact he has a Menzian preference for not being beholden to the big end of town and, while clearly he has to deal with it, has markedly distanced himself from the big business/big government/big unions corporatist model which characterised government in the Hawke and Keating years.

It seems obvious to me that Howard realises he has a variety of constituencies to attend to and larger responsibilities that go with prime ministerial office, and that's what he concentrates on. Rundle's summation of a recent drugs strategy is that "by insisting on familial pieties, the federal campaign offered a black, comic allegory of John Howard's incomprehension of the contemporary world". At his best, Guy Rundle understands that there is no such single entity as "the contemporary world". Howard knows full well that the people who keep on electing him live in a plurality of sometimes overlapping conceptual worlds. It's the disquieting ease with which Howard intuits the ways people who are quite unlike him think and feel and can be persuaded which provoked Rundle into this bewildered and, despite itself, mesmerised tract.

Christopher Pearson

THE OPPORTUNIST | Correspondence

One Victory for the Battlers over the Elites
Tony Walker

First published in the *Australian Financial Review*, 16 November 2001.

Funny thing how the Howard ascendancy is being framed as a victory over the "élites" or is it "aylites". Since the election we have heard a lot about this ill-defined group on the basis that John Howard prevailed in spite of the enmity of the so-called élites. The assumption among those using this pejorative is that what emerged from the election was the authentic voice of Australia in contrast with élite (read media) opinion which is out of touch.

Apart from the self-righteousness and arrogance inherent in this point of view (where does the truth really lie?) it is also dangerous because it assumes division between discrete groups which may not even exist in any well-defined way. For example, this newspaper [*Australian Financial Review*], which might be regarded as a vehicle for élite opinion aimed at an élite market, editorialised in favour of returning the Howard Government on the basis that the alternative had not made a compelling case for change. So much for the media's commanding heights being captured by the anti-Howard élites!

Of course, the assault on the élites is a continuation of criticism of "political correctness" and the allegedly boilerplate views of the "commentariat". To that critique we have a new word which has inserted itself into the political lexicon: "moralisers".

We'll come back to that. Out of the mouths of Howard's triumphalist cohort since the election has come a steady invective against the so-called élites on the basis presumably that if the spoils of battle go to the victor, so does the opportunity to write its preliminary history. What we journalists call the first rough draft (of history), and rough it is in this case.

All this reminds me of the nearly ten years I spent as a correspondent in China where pejorative words are indeed lethal weapons politically. Thus, Mao Zedong, the educated son of a well-to-do grain merchant and a privileged Chinese by any standards, railed against "élites" (in Chinese, *shangliu*: literally, "upstream" or less literally, "highbrow").

Actually, Mao had a long list of "enemies of the people" including landlords, rightists, bad elements and his catch-all during the Cultural Revolution, the "stinking ninth". This was the ninth category of class enemies and included more than a few members of my own profession who found themselves cleaning out cowsheds and pigsties, or something worse.

This columnist is certainly not suggesting Howard's assault on the "élites", however that group might be defined, is cause for any particular concern, beyond arguing that assailing and branding particular groups in society seems pretty pointless unless the aim is to further deepen divisions … or sow discord.

It might also be pointed out that Howard himself can hardly say he is not a member of an élite. If a prime minister with a law degree, a million-dollar superannuation fund and a well-stocked wine cellar in a mansion with harbour views is not a member of an élite I don't know who is.

Howard preaches against the "politics of envy" and yet he aligns himself with the "battlers" against what he described after the election in a revealing aside as "big everything". Now there is nothing wrong with a neo-conservative politician portraying himself as a "man of the people", if he can get away with it. After all, Ronald Reagan did the same thing while remaining a fully paid-up member of the West Coast élite.

This is clever politics, but the essential difference between Howard and Reagan is that the latter's success was based on his geniality and inclusiveness. Reagan might have practised wedge politics, but these were wedges in velvet gloves. Howard's wedges are something else, which prompts this thought: live by the wedge, die by the wedge.

But back to the "moralisers" which is, of course, a coded attack on people critical of the Government's policy on asylum seekers. These include two former Liberal leaders, Malcolm Fraser and John Hewson, along with Treasurer Peter Costello's brother, Tim, who are being depicted as the "moralisers-in-chief". The argument here appears to be that not only are the moralisers completely out of touch with the mainstream, even worse they are part of the dreaded élites.

If the argument is that morality is an imperfect standard to judge what is right and wrong, that is an entirely reasonable proposition. But if those who adopt moral positions are abused simply for having done so because it is politically inconvenient, that is something else altogether.

Tony Walker

THE OPPORTUNIST | *Response to correspondence*

Guy Rundle

Who is John Howard? That is the question that arose, somewhat improbably, during the election campaign. It is a question that will always haunt conservatives who move in the milieu of cosmopolitan political worlds – if you really are one of the silent majority, why aren't you down here with us, doing the nine-to-five and tending your lawn? Nixon was the politician who embodied this conundrum most markedly – the man whom Hunter Thompson dubbed as the essence of everything "plastic and sexless" about the modern world, yet with the saturnine glamour, the hint that something darker lay beneath the surface. Thompson wasn't the only one to spill a lot of ink trying to work out who Nixon was.

Howard never seemed like that sort of bloke. Never the Metternichian breaker of nations or the sleazy cold warrior, he seemed to be the improbable arrival of an actual representative of the far-flung brick veneer. One of the first mentions of him was as one of the two Liberal ops in the Loans Affair – a "former suburban solicitor" locked in a motel with Tirath Khemlani to go through the documents. That view has been pretty commonly accepted since – whatever his sins may be, Howard was a true believer in the liberal-conservative vision. Indeed in 1987 his tenure as head of the Opposition was white-anted by a near-consensus view that his leadership was not merely poor, but a category error – a judgement (unfair, but self-perpetuating) that gave the Joh-for-Canberra movement its window of opportunity. He seemed to believe it himself – "Lazarus with a triple bypass" was a flash of wit that seemed to come out of relief: he no longer had to pretend to be anything more than a lieutenant.

The *Tampa* crisis made more visible what has always been a minority view of Howard – that he is a far more cynical, flexible and dexterous politician than people have been willing to admit, and that those who underestimate him – Peacock and Kennett to judge by their car-phone transcripts – do so at their peril. I am of that minority – although other members of it include people such as Paul Keating and Bob Ellis. Having dipped deeply into Howard's historical record for the essay and having contemplated his public persona over the years while writing satirical takes on the man for Max Gillies I am in no doubt that Howard can turn his performance on a sixpence. That he believes the act makes it all the easier for him.

Yes, Howard has a specific set of values – he's no Andrew Peacock, though his recent behaviour has led some to compare him to Billy Hughes. But lack of content is neither the most common form of opportunism nor the most successful. The true opportunist, the true political professional, knows that he has a certain range that he shouldn't go out of, and looks for opportune times at which to let rip. When things go bad he keeps his head down and his powder dry. The true believer, by contrast, comes out with all guns blazing whatever conditions may prevail. Who would be examples of the latter type from the conservative side – leaving aside the question of their actual concrete beliefs? Enoch Powell might be one. He was not above a certain manipulativeness, but he was willing to follow his beliefs wherever they led him – ultimately out of the Conservative party and into the (Ulster) Unionist one, urging people to vote Labour in order to keep Britain out of the EEC. Closer to home, Steele Hall – who voted himself out of office in South Australia by abandoning Playford's gerrymander in the late '60s – would be an example, albeit more from the genuinely liberal wing.

The difference between these men and Howard is that they did not believe in success at all costs – they were aware that such conduct could do greater damage to their own cause or to the social and political whole than was worth any advantage they could gain by pursuing it. Howard and his government have taken the opposite course. Coming from a party which purports to value liberal political institutions and to understand their fragility, the Howard era has been one in which such institutions have been treated with a systematic contempt unparalleled at the federal level within the last sixty years. The waterfront dispute, the *Border Protection Act* and the relentless attack on the judiciary for "political" – i.e. decisions the government doesn't like – rulings have treated parliament with a contempt that has genuinely weakened it. Parliament is hardly the perfect expression of true self-rule, especially in a society with such narrow media ownership, but it is what you might call "actually existing freedom" – some protection against the expansion of executive power. The more it is undermined, the harder it is to re-establish its authority. That someone from the "non-parliamentary" Left should need to defend it is a measure of how far and dangerously to the right things have drifted, and the lack of concern that those who purport to be "liberals" have for it at present.

The opportunism that Howard has shown towards these institutions seems to me to be all but unarguable.

More speculative is the question of Howard's view on the issues of border security and asylum seekers. As many have pointed out, he was one of the few to vote against any special generosity being shown to the boat people arriving from Vietnam in the '70s and '80s. But I don't believe for a second that Howard really thinks there is a refugee crisis. Up to the time of the *Tampa* the Coalition's management of ship-based arrivals had been virtually identical to that of the ALP, which had pioneered the policy of detention. That a refugee campaign gathered steam in the last couple of years is due to global rather than local events – if Beazley had won in 1998 his policy wouldn't have significantly differed from the pre-*Tampa* approach of Howard. I doubt that Howard has much sympathy or under-standing for the plight of asylum seekers, but he can crunch the numbers well enough, which is why no *Border Protection Act* was brought in to deal with the several dozen ships that arrived prior to the *Tampa*. With the *Tampa* he had a godsend – a ship that would never sink and could be kept in limbo indefinitely while the shock jocks went to work on a populace given a wholly false picture of the refugee "problem".

That sort of footwork marks the opportunist off from the true believer. Look at the way the immigration debate flared in the 1980s, when Howard dropped in a couple of sly comments and then withdrew, Cheshire Cat-style, as the barney erupted. Compare the conduct of then-Senator John Stone who called a horticultural soil-inversion tool a goddamn shovel and said flat out that – in his opinion – you'd be mad not to reduce Asian immigration. Howard is prime minister, Stone lost his lower house seat bid and then tried to crawl his way back on to the National Party Senate ticket and is now out of the game. Those simple skills – knowing how much to say, when to say it and when to shut up –

are enough to mark the man who is always thinking strategically about his own values.

In that respect it is always surprising the degree to which he manages to attract those who want to see him as a gold-standard representative of a certain naïve and unreflected-upon cultural position. In this respect I'd suggest that John Birmingham has fallen into the trap that Howard has semi-consciously set. Yes, Howard is relentless, yes he's tenacious, but he is as operationally insincere as any politician needs to be. He's perfected the art of simply walking away from a position he held by saying he was wrong and there's an end to the matter – as he did with his accusation that Nelson Mandela was the head of a terrorist organisation, with his commitment to abolishing Medicare, and with the apotheosis of all this, the invention of "core" and "non-core" promises. By relentlessly drumming the image of mateship, egalitarianism and the battlers, he presents himself as the distilled essence of working and lower-middle-class Australia. But to believe this projection is to fall for the idea that there is an Australian essence that can be captured in a man, to believe that the digger spirit is of necessity fused with a certain set of social attitudes. Where does this leave someone like Tom Uren – Japanese POW, socialist and anti-war activist? To believe that he refuses an apology because he believes in "practical reconciliation" (i.e. virtual assimilation) is to fall for the soft sell. The man who can weep tears for the death of a famous cricketer yet can spare none for a people whose bones his culture was built on is a man who lacks a compassionate imagination, and shows no sign of wanting to get one. As Tony Walker notes, Howard – and various cohorts – has been monumentally successful in selling the idea of an "élite" who are somehow not real Australians and who apparently have no right to interfere in the society of the "real" Aussies. Doubtless Birmingham has had as much experience as I of dumb self-satisfied inner-city people whose mission in life seems to be confirm such caricatures. Exasperation can often send you back to the Howard-style message and obscure the fact that it's a tactically planned cultural war.

Although, according to Christopher Pearson, it is Howard who has always been on the defensive in a cultural war. Space precludes a full response to Pearson's belief that ship-borne asylum seekers represent a security threat; suffice to say that you don't have to be of the Left to find it barely rational. The division over the handling of the refugee issue has not occurred along the left-right divide – it runs through deep right territory, with people such as Greg Sheridan, Paul Kelly and John Hewson – vegan anarcho-Trotskyists all – regarding it much as the Left does, as an unsubstantiated moral panic. Yes, there may well be criminals among the general refugee population. No one seriously denies that a small number of young and middle-aged male arrivals may need to be detained. The fact that this is not the primary purpose of detention is evidenced by the fact that women, children and old men are dealt the same treatment. Refugees may coalesce into gangs? What better way to catalyse the process than by grouping them in camps where the ruthless can establish their rule? Terrorists coming through the years-long process of asylum seeking? There may be an example of a terrorist incident in the west caused by an asylum seeker, but I don't know of one. The vast majority of foreign terrorists (and gangsters) fly first-class and are far more likely to come in on the business migration program than on a plank floating into Flying Fish cove. The risk – vanishingly small compared to life's real risks – is simply one of the conditions of globalisation and new degrees of global mobility. Pearson's charge that I do not consider the national interest is particularly awry – you only have to look at the editorials of the *Economist* and *Wall Street Journal*, not to mention the Asian press, to see what long-term damage mucking about with boats has done to our standing close to home and further abroad. Indeed that is the key point that writers like Sheridan and Kelly are making. Dispute it if you wish, but don't claim a monopoly on strategic thinking.

Pearson gets tangled on this because he wants to paint me as a disdainer of Howard – hence his belief that I am being "snobbish" about the dorkiness of Howard's walkabout photo-ops. But clearly I was not talking about the fact of that – undeniable and widely accepted – dorkiness, merely about the visual images associated with the Howard era and the way in which the *Tampa* pseudo-crisis swept them away. If Pearson doesn't believe that even Howard's political supporters find him to be drab and nerdy, then he is truly a loyal retainer. He needs to be blind to the way in which Howard has constituted a political persona, and that involves a certain blindness to the analytical skepticism of those who suss Howard – he prefers to believe instead that I simply hate the man from a position within the élites. When you start down that track, you can believe all the fictions that "post-modern" conservatism throws up, from the televisual reconstitution of the family via the drugs campaign (if the family is the seat of moral authority, why do we need to impose such authority via TV?) to the primal threat of the encroaching brown and yellow hordes.

Guy Rundle

John Birmingham is the author of *Leviathan*, a history of Sydney. His essay *Appeasing Jakarta* was the second in the *Quarterly Essay* series.

Paul Bongiorno is Network Ten's Parliament House bureau chief in Canberra. He has been the presenter of Network Ten's national political program *Meet the Press* since 1996.

Christopher Pearson is the editor of the *Adelaide Review*, a columnist for the *Australian Financial Review* and a member of the Australia Council and the Council of the National Museum of Australia.

Guy Rundle is the co-editor of *Arena* magazine, a magazine of political and social comment, and the writer of *Your Dreaming*, the latest political satire from Max Gillies. He is a regular essayist for the *Age* and the *Sydney Morning Herald*.

Tony Walker is chief political correspondent for the *Australian Financial Review*.

Don Watson lives in Fitzroy with his wife Hilary McPhee. A former academic historian, he wrote satire for Max Gillies in the eighties, and went on to speechwriting, a profession he practised until the fall of the Keating government in 1996. Watson has also written screenplays (*Passion* and *The Man Who Sued God*) and a number of books, including *The Story of Australia*. His *Recollections of a Bleeding Heart: A Portrait of the Keating Government*, is to be published by Random House in 2002.

QUARTERLY ESSAY

SUBSCRIPTION

This festive season, surprise a friend with a subscription to Quarterly Essay...

Receive a discount and never miss an issue. Mailed direct to your door. 1 year subscription (4 issues): $34.95 a year within Australia inc. GST (Institutional subs. $40). Outside Australia $70.

PAYMENT DETAILS I enclose a cheque/money order made out to Schwartz Publishing. Please debit my credit card (Mastercard, Visa Card or Bankcard accepted).

Card No. ☐☐☐☐☐☐☐☐☐☐☐☐☐☐☐☐

Expiry date   /

Cardholder's name

Signature

Name

Address

POST OR FAX TO:
Black Inc.
Level 3, 167 Collins Street, Melbourne,
Victoria 3000 Australia
Telephone: 61 3 9654 2000
Facsimile: 61 3 9654 2290
Email: quarterlyessay@blackincbooks.com